Wake Up the Mighty Men

*Children are like arrows
in the hands of a mighty man...*

Unless otherwise indicated all Scripture quotations are from the *King James Version* of the Bible.

Scripture quotations marked Phillips are taken from the *New Testament in Modern English* (Rev. Ed.) by J. B. Phillips. Copyright © 1958, 1960, 1972 by J. B. Phillips. Reprinted by permission of Macmillan Publishing Co., New York, New York.

Scripture quotations marked AMP are taken from *The Amplified Bible. Old Testament* copyright © 1965, 1987 by Zondervan Corporation, Grand Rapids, Michigan. *New Testament* copyright © 1958, 1987 by The Lockman Foundation, La Habra, California. Used by permission.

Scripture quotations marked NASB are taken from the *New American Standard Bible.* Copyright © The Lockman Foundation 1960, 1962, 1963, 1968, 1971, 1972, 1973, 1975, 1977. Used by permission.

Cover design and execution by sigma graphic design, Wichita, Kansas.

Wake Up the Mighty Men
Children are like arrows
in the hands of a mighty man...
ISBN 0-9667234-0-6
Copyright © 1998 by Rich and Kathy Hartman
8177 S. Harvard, Suite 727
Tulsa, Oklahoma 74137

Printed in the United States of America.
All rights reserved under International Copyright Law. Contents and/or cover may not be reproduced in whole or in part in any form without the express written consent of the Publisher.

Wake Up the Mighty Men

*Children are like arrows
in the hands of a mighty man...*

by

Rich and Kathy Hartman

Contents

Dedication		7
Acknowledgments		9
Foreword		11
Preface		13
Chapter 1	Children Are Ministers	17
Chapter 2	Make Them Welcome	27
Chapter 3	Standing on the Word and Pouring in the Oil	33
Chapter 4	No Praisey, Go Crazy	45
Chapter 5	Wisdom	53
Chapter 6	The Whack	61
Chapter 7	No Work, No Eat	73
Chapter 8	Watch the Watch	81
Chapter 9	Hitting the Bull's-eye	91
Chapter 10	Willingness	107
References		110
About the Authors		111

Dedication

We dedicate this book to Elizabeth Sherman, not only because she edited it, but for being an inspiration as a single mom who has succeeded in training up two world changers.

Acknowledgments

Thank you, Steve and Leanna Willis, for doing such a great job on the cover.

Thank you, Kelly James, for patiently plowing through the first edit — deciphering Rich's "unique" penmanship!

Thank you, Scott Williams, for believing in us and getting behind this project wholeheartedly.

Thank you, Pastor Bob Yandian, our pastor for seventeen years, for the solid foundation of the Word of God you placed under us.

Thank you, Carman, for the challenge, exhortation, and encouragement to step out in faith and follow our calling and the vision God placed in our hearts.

Thank you, Pastor Mark Derksen, for constantly praying for us, encouraging us, and staying on top of all we're doing.

Thank you, Tim Storey, for being a friend and mentor.

And thank you to our board, who have stuck with us through thick and thin, praying for us and giving us wise counsel during some very difficult times: Bob and Dee Mongraine, Jan and Phil Calvert, and Carman Licciardello.

Foreword

God is raising up a new generation of world shakers and history makers, people who will make a maximum impact on this generation. I thank God that Rich and Kathy Hartman are two of the new world shakers. Their ministry to children and adults alike is both refreshing and on the cutting edge of what God is doing.

Rich and Kathy's new book takes you from the promise, principle, and power, into the proof of an exciting life in Jesus Christ.

Way to go, Rich and Kathy!

This book is dynamic reading — enjoy!

Tim Storey

Preface

In November of 1982 the Holy Spirit gave first to me and then later to Kathy a scripture from Isaiah:

> **And they that shall be of thee shall build the old waste places: thou shalt raise up the foundations of many generations; and thou shalt be called, The repairer of the breach, The restorer of paths to dwell in.**
> **Isaiah 58:12**

At the time, it made little sense. Then on November 20, 1983, at about 4:00 in the morning, the Holy Spirit woke me, saying, "Prepare for war." It was so clear and so strong, I immediately woke Kathy and said, "God just told me to prepare for war."

She asked, "What did He mean — spiritual or natural?"

I said, "I don't know. He didn't say. He just said, 'Prepare for war.'"

That evening at our home church, Jerry Savelle was the guest speaker. When he began his message, he said, "Open your Bibles to Joel 3:9." He proceeded to read:

> Proclaim ye this among the Gentiles; Prepare war, wake up the mighty men, let all the men of war draw near; let them come up.

The Lord was confirming the message He'd given me earlier that morning and adding to it. He said, "Prepare for war. Wake up the mighty men."

In truth, Kathy and I were some of the first "mighty men" to wake up. We had not been in children's ministry for very long, but one of the scriptures we were led to share with teachers and parents again and again was:

> As arrows are in the hand of a mighty man; so are children of the youth.
>
> Psalm 127:4

It was all beginning to fit together. Through Isaiah 58:12, God gave us the vision — Repair and restore families. Then Joel 3:9 told us how to carry it out — Wake up the mighty men and women of the Body of Christ with this message: *God has given children in their care for the purpose of forming and aiming them as His arrows to destroy Satan's kingdom in spiritual battle.*

Kathy and I presently have ten children and ten grandchildren. We have ministered to thousands of kids, their parents, and their Sunday school and children's church teachers for many years now. We travel across the country and around the world teaching children that they are gifts in the Church and giving them the opportunity to move in those gifts. At the same time, we teach their parents and teachers how to recognize and nurture those gifts.

We are grateful for the tremendous work of organizations like Promise Keepers. As these men become the husbands and fathers God calls them to be, they are the fulfillment of Malachi 4:5,6 in these last days:

Preface

> Behold, I will send you Elijah the prophet before the coming of the great and dreadful day of the Lord:
> And he shall turn the heart of the fathers to the children, and the heart of the children to their fathers, lest I come and smite the earth with a curse.

I had the honor of witnessing the restoration of Jim Bakker and his son, Jamie, at Pastor Tommy Barnett's church in Phoenix, Arizona. As tears streamed down our faces, we knew we were seeing a prototype of the restoration God will be performing in more and more families all over the world as Jesus' appearing draws closer.

Our prayer is that this book will be another tool for the Holy Spirit to use to wake up adults in the Body of Christ to see the importance of ministering to a child — whether that child is in their own home, their neighborhood, goes to their church, or lives in their community.

These mighty men and women will get out of bed, rise up, and correct wrongs in their homes and in the local children's church. They will build on the areas that have been correctly established, direct their arrows (children) to the bull's-eye (Jesus), stir up their children's gifts and callings — and thereby be blessed.

Our motto is, "Train up adults in the way they should go, and then they'll be able to train up children in the way they should go!"

Chapter 1

Children Are Ministers

> **And he gave some,** (the *Phillips Translation* says, "Some he made") **apostles; and some, prophets; and some, evangelists; and some, pastors and teachers; For the perfecting of the saints, for the work of the ministry, for the edifying of the body of Christ.**
>
> **Ephesians 4:11,12**

In this verse we want to emphasize **the perfecting of the saints, for the work of the ministry.**

The Holy Spirit tells us it is God who defines and appoints these ministry offices. Next, He lists the offices or ministry gifts and tells us why God gave them. The Greek word translated **perfecting** is a medical term meaning "the setting of a bone." God gave the ministry offices to set the members of the Body of Christ in their proper places.

This remedy is expressed in Psalm 107:20, [God] **sent his word, and healed them.** God gave the ministry gifts to heal broken, out-of-joint souls with His Word, and then those healed will heal others by using the Word that healed them. Essentially, ministry is a duplication process.

Notice, God sent His Word to "heal" sheep, not to "beat" them. Psalm 23:4 says that His rod comforts. This is an attitude we should cling to. Please don't join the S.B.A. (Sheep Beaters Anonymous)!

> ...the perfecting of the *saints*, for the work of the ministry [italics mine].

Who are the saints? The average mindset is, "Anyone older than children." But does God see it that way? No! In Matthew 19: 14,15 Jesus said,

> **Suffer** (permit or choose to allow) **little children, and forbid them not, to come unto me: for of such is the kingdom of heaven. And he laid his hands on them, and departed thence.**

The *New American Standard Bible* says, **Let the children alone.** The Greek word for **suffer** actually means "a commitment to a decision which will result in an effective choice" or "picking up an arrow aimed in the wrong direction and redirecting it to its proper target." In other words, you are making a decision that will bear fruit. Many times, Peter, James, and John acted like the three stooges. In one particular episode (Matthew 19:14) they were shooing the children away from Jesus.

I can just hear the disciples saying, "Don't bother Him. He's busy teaching BIG church. He's got more important things to do than to be concerned with you. And besides, you couldn't understand Him anyway." Jesus turned and lovingly said to His disciples, "Would you guys just chill? I've put in their hearts a desire to seek Me!" (Hartman translation.)

It reminds me of the W. C. Fields line, "Go away, little boy, you bother me!" **Forbid them not** in the Greek actually means "do not stop an action that is already in progress." In other words, Jesus was saying, "Guys, I've put a desire in their hearts to seek Me. They are a spirit and spirit can only communicate with spirit."

Watch for Falling Rocks

As I was teaching this in Mexico City at a pastor's conference, I asked the Lord how I could convey this thought with clarity so the pastors there could really understand and remember. He gave me this picture: There was a large mountain behind the church. If someone at the top of the mountain pushed a boulder down the mountain, it would be stupid to stand in its path. It's not going to stop! In fact, you would look like a moron if you stood in its way.

In the same way, God is saying "Don't be stupid! Do not stand between Me and a child, but make a decision to encourage them to come and bring them to Me. Bring them into a relationship with Me." God has put a desire in the heart of every child to seek Him, to have a personal relationship with Him.

This idea is further backed up in Psalm 128:3, which says that a child is like an olive plant, and many other passages compare a son to a flower. Just as a plant naturally leans toward the sun, a child naturally — or should we say supernaturally — leans toward the Son (Jesus).

When I was a boy, I would trick my mother's plants, which were always bending toward the window. I would turn them around, pointing them toward the interior of the room. Within twenty-four hours they would be bent back to the window — and the sunlight. In the same way, children naturally, or supernaturally, bend toward the Sonlight.

Born to Seek God

Jesus was saying in Matthew 19:14,15 that He put a desire in the hearts of children to seek Him. But just like my mom's house plants, if you continue to direct the child toward darkness, they will eventually die spiritually. We have heard the story that an evangelist friend of ours has personally ministered the plan of salvation to Yassir Arafat. As of this date, Yassir has said, "No, sir" to God. It is our friend's prayer, as well as ours, that Yassir will say "Yes, sir" to Father God someday.

You see, in the heart of Yassir Arafat is a God-given desire to seek Him and to have a spirit-to-spirit relationship. Even Adolph Hitler was born with a desire to seek God and have a relationship with the Holy Spirit. In the heart of Saddam Hussein is a desire to have a relationship with the Holy Spirit. What happened in those men's lives? It is my belief that the adults who were in their sphere of influence when they were children did not pick them up as arrows and aim or direct them toward God.

People want a relationship with God. He created us with the desire to know Him, but since man can't see God, he tends to follow what he can see. This is well illustrated in 1 Samuel, where the people of Israel demanded that Samuel appoint a king over them, just as the heathens had. They wanted a leader whom they could see with their eyes. They did not trust that God was leading them, because they could not see Him. They were weak in faith.

The apostle Paul understood this principle. He told the Corinthian church in 1 Corinthians 11:1:

> Be ye followers of me, even as I also am of Christ.

Paul was an example, someone they could see. Paul was saying, "Follow me as I follow Jesus, but don't follow me if I'm not following Jesus."

Battle for the Mind

Why are kids drawn to the Ninja Turtles, Mighty Morphin Power Rangers, Dungeons and Dragons, MTV, rock music, cults, and the occult? Because the world has been smarter than many of us by learning how to captivate their minds, which Proverbs 11:30 tells us to do. Through new-age cartoons, role-playing games, music, and other media, they are teaching our children about spirit-to-spirit communication — with the wrong spirit!

Years ago Kathy and I watched two episodes of the Smurfs. On one occasion, they were levitating objects in the name of Beelzebub, which Matthew 12:24 says is Satan, the lord of the flies. In another episode they were mocking Noah and called God a "know-nothing." The world is aggressively teaching our children about the spirit world, the real world — from the devil's perspective.

We have been in several Pentecostal churches where we've been asked not to lead the children in the baptism of the Holy Spirit. This is frustrating to us, because the following scriptures say,

> They that worship [God] must worship him in spirit and in truth.
> **John 4:24**

> For he that speaketh in an unknown tongue speaketh not unto men, but unto God.
> **1 Corinthians 14:2**

> Having a form of godliness, but denying the power thereof: from such turn away.
> **2 Timothy 3:5**

The Greek word for **form** means "an outline of, or resemblance of." This verse reminds me of detective shows where a line is painted on the ground outlining where the murdered body was found. Religion has a form or outline of Jesus, but the body isn't there. This picture tells us that the power that raised Jesus from the dead, the power of the Holy Spirit, is absent and is being denied. The outline or form is there, but no live body!

There are those who will say, "No Holy Spirit power allowed. Give children a form of Jesus, but don't lead them to the power that raised Jesus from the dead." But it is the power of the Holy Spirit in their life, a relationship with the Holy Spirit, that they are desiring. God put that desire in them.

As Kathy and I travel across the United States and to other countries, it has been our desire to teach children that they can communicate with the Holy Spirit. In our years of local church and road ministry, we have seen thousands of children receive the infilling of the Holy Spirit with the evidence of speaking in tongues and begin communicating with God. (See 1 Corinthians 14.)

I believe this is important to God, because He devotes many chapters in His Word to the subject of the Holy Spirit and His role in our lives. Children need and want the Holy Spirit, and God wants them to receive Him and even operate in His gifts.

Supernatural Kids

In November of 1990, we were ministering in a church in Crystal Springs, Mississippi. After the altar call, I began to lay hands on children who had come up to receive their prayer language. As I started at one end of the line, a little six-year-old girl at the other end of the line began to weep, laugh, shake, and speak in tongues.

This little girl had submitted herself to the Holy Spirit on her own. Then, on her own, she turned around and began laying hands on several other children, who also received their prayer language.

Too Young?

When Kathy and I were going through three days of intense attack from the enemy, we got a call from friends who pastor a church in Minnesota. They told us that their their one-and-a-half-year-old son, Josiah, had told his mom and dad throughout the day, "Pray for Rich and Kathy." Praise God! Josiah was sensitive to the Holy Spirit. His parents had encouraged him and directed him to a relationship with the Holy Spirit. They didn't mock him or take lightly his "childlike faith."

In August of 1991, we were ministering at their church. One afternoon, the pastor and his wife had gone to run some errands. They left Kathy and me to look after Josiah, who was not yet three years old. God spoke to Kathy and told her, "I'm going to fill Josiah with the Holy Spirit tonight."

That evening, I did an altar call for the infilling of the Holy Spirit. Josiah's hand shot up, he came down for prayer, and he received his prayer language. The pastor and his wife have told us that he continues to pray in tongues daily. It's a way of life for him.

Our own daughter, Destinee, received Jesus and her prayer language at two and a half years old, and by the time she was three God was already performing miracles of healing through her as she prayed for people. Once she saw angels hovering over Kenneth Copeland's jet, and she was given a word of knowledge last year.

One summer we were ministering to children at a pastors' conference in Texas. Five different children gave tongues, interpretations, exhortations, and words of knowledge. While we were at a four-day camp in Colorado, the Lord revealed Himself to many children. At the end of an already powerful session, angels appeared to five children on separate occasions. They said the angels talked to them and encouraged them.

Another pastor friend of ours was ministering in Arkansas several years ago, where he met a little girl who astounded him. One day she told her mom and dad, "I'm going to have a baby sister. Her name will be Kara."

Her mother and father were astonished, and asked her where she got this information. She told them that an angel had told her. Within a month, her mother discovered she was pregnant. Nine months later, the little girl knocked on her parents bedroom door and said, "Kara's coming tonight!" Within hours, her mother delivered a little girl, and guess what they named the baby? Kara, of course!

While still on staff as children's pastors at Grace Fellowship in Tulsa, Oklahoma, I gave a tongue. Then the Lord impressed me that one of the children had the interpretation. As I was encouraging the children to operate in the gift of interpretation, a twelve-year-old boy stood up and spoke the interpretation. It was right on. His teacher and I were amazed. This was a boy who was always in trouble in children's church, because he came from an environment of physical and verbal abuse. It confirmed to Kathy and me that we are not to focus on the natural, but to see children as God sees them, by the Spirit.

Can children hear from God? YES! God has put in children's hearts a desire to seek Him and know Him, to have a spirit-to-spirit relationship. But they also must be "trained and aimed"!

My Sheep Know My Voice

Children can learn to recognize God's voice, the voice of their Shepherd. Sheep herders say that several herds can be drinking or grazing together, and when one shepherd calls his sheep, only his sheep come. The sheep know their shepherd's voice. Jesus said His sheep would know His voice. (See John 10.) When you encourage children to listen, they'll begin to hear God and not listen to the voice of a stranger.

> **And a stranger will they not follow, but will flee from him: for they know not the voice of strangers.**
>
> **John 10:5**

The bottom line is: In Matthew 19:14, Jesus said (Hartman translation), "Do not stop an action already in progress. I have put in these children a desire to seek Me, a desire to communicate with Me, and a desire to have a relationship with the Holy Spirit."

> **And it shall come to pass afterward, that I will pour out my spirit upon all flesh; and your sons and your daughters shall prophesy, your old men shall dream dreams, your young men shall see visions.**
>
> **Joel 2:28**

That means children too!

I have heard Willie George teach that Samson is a picture of the end-time church. He spoke of how Samson fell, subsequently repented, and though blinded, was led to the temple by a little boy, where he proceeded to push the pillars over. He destroyed more Philistines in that one day than he had in his whole lifetime.

God has shown Kathy and me that this "last days" revival will be ushered in by the young and old together — not adults alone, and not children alone. We are going to see the fulfillment of God's promise that the hearts of the fathers and sons, as well as the mothers and daughters, will become one in serving the Lord.

Prayer of Commitment

Father God, in Jesus' name I ask You to forgive me for having a W. C. Fields mentality. I ask You to show me how to lead those little ones in my sphere of influence to a relationship with You, with Jesus, and with the Holy Spirit. Amen.

Chapter 2

Make Them Welcome

In Isaiah 28:9 the Holy Spirit reveals to us who can understand the deep things of God. It says,

> Whom shall he teach knowledge? and whom shall he make to understand doctrine? them that are weaned from the milk, and drawn from the breasts.
> Isaiah 28:9

Jesus saw children as part of the Body of Christ.

In 1 Corinthians 11:29,30, the communion passage, we are told that our physical body is sick because we've not discerned the Lord's Body properly. The Greek word for **discerned** means "to see clearly, to take a proper view of, to form a just estimate of value."

Yes, God is talking about sin, but He is also telling us that we need to discern our part in the Body. How do we know 1 Corinthians 11 is referring to our roles in Jesus' Body? Because the next chapter, 1 Corinthians 12, talks about the gifts and different members placed in His Body, the Church.

Again, children are part of the Body of Christ. Therefore, we must ask ourselves: Do we clearly see their role and value? Do we have a proper view of them? *Do we have a just estimate of their value as Jesus does?*

God is telling us to open our spiritual eyes. As we have learned in the previous chapter, children want a relationship with God. He put the desire in them. We saw how Jesus exhorted His disciples, "My Body cannot function properly without the children. Do not stop them from coming to Me."

> Whosoever therefore shall humble himself as this little child, the same is greatest in the kingdom of heaven. And whoso shall receive one such little child in my name receiveth me.
>
> Matthew 18:4,5

The word **receive** in the Greek means "to make one feel like a welcome guest." Jesus said to make a child feel like a welcome guest. To help clarify this, let's look at Psalm 22:3, which says that God inhabits, lives in, or dwells in our praises.

> But thou art holy, O thou that inhabitest the praises of Israel.

I have always wondered, *Why does God say He lives in our praises when He's already in us?* We are the temple of the Holy Spirit. More than that, God is omnipresent. King David said, "Even if I were in Sheol (hell) God would be there." (See Psalm 139:8.) He is Jehovah Shammah, our omnipresent God Who guides us and guards us.

The answer lies in the Hebrew meaning of the word **inhabit**. It means "to make someone feel like a welcome guest." Yes, God is always in our temple, but when we praise Him, He is not only there, but He is *at home* there. He feels welcome and comfortable.

When we praise and worship God, we are not restraining Him from being Himself in any way. God can be God! And John 10:10 tells us His character, what He's really like. He comes to give life — the more abundant life. So when we praise Him, He can do whatever He wants in our temple, giving us whatever we need in life in abundance!

As Kathy and I travel, we often stay in homes of people we don't know or are barely acquainted with. We are in their homes, but we don't feel "at home." It's not their fault. We just don't have a close relationship with them. It's not the same as staying at a good friend's home.

We have friends in Tulsa who are like family. We feel comfortable getting some milk out of their refrigerator or borrowing their toothpaste. The difference between staying with people we hardly know and staying with our friends is that we have a close relationship with our friends. We are completely at ease in their presence.

So Jesus is saying that, just as God is welcome and free to be Himself in our temple as we praise Him, children are free to open up and receive Him and His Word when we have a heart attitude that makes them feel at home in our presence.

We need to build such a relationship with the children around us, whether they are our own or those in our church and community. We want them to feel totally at home in our presence. We should strive to know them by name, know their dog's name, and ask how their Aunt Susie is. And by making them feel totally welcome in our presence, we have made Jesus welcome too!

When Jesus is at home in you, your home, and your church, He can be Himself. Then, as the Holy Spirit wills, He can give you words of knowledge for the children, the gift of faith may operate, healings and miracles can take place, and so on. You will see God's anointing flowing through you for the child's sake. You will see the power of God revealed to them through you. *Make them welcome and you've made Jesus welcome.*

Don't Bait the Trap

> But whoso shall offend one of these little ones which believe in me, it were better for him that a millstone were hanged about his neck, and that he were drowned in the depth of the sea.
>
> Matthew 18:6

The word **offend** is the Greek word *skandalizo*, which is where we get the words "scandal" and "scandalize." It literally means "to entice, or to put bait on the trigger of a trap; for the purpose of enticing, as to snare and kill."

As a little boy, I remember setting mouse traps by putting cheese or peanut butter on the tripper to entice a mouse. I was directing that mouse toward his own destruction with the bait. The next morning, we'd find a dead mouse.

In this verse of Scripture, God is painting us a picture of our heart attitude. In Matthew 18:5 He says, "Make them feel welcome," and in verse 6 He says, "But if you don't, you are baiting a trap and enticing them to be destroyed spiritually. Not only will they be destroyed spiritually, but so will you."

Literally, Jesus describes how the spirit of antichrist operates in this world, enticing children — and adults — into destruction and eternal damnation. And the bait is everything from occultic cartoons to humanistic education.

To take this a step further, let's consider Who Jesus is. He is the Christ, the anointed One, the One Who has given the Holy Spirit (the anointing) to His Body. Now let's consider antichrist, who is opposed to the anointed One and opposed to the anointing. The devil will use every enticement and every trick he can think of to keep children from God and the anointing.

> **And fear not them which kill the body, but are not able to kill the soul: but rather fear him which is able to destroy both soul and body in hell.**
> **Matthew 10:28**

Why are kids shooting kids? Someone has set a trap to destroy their soul and send them to hell and those kids have swallowed the bait.

Can these atrocities be stopped? Absolutely! We must receive and make welcome the children. Then Jesus feels welcome and will move in on the scene as we share Him with them.

Just remember, don't hang a millstone around your neck and go for a swim! Don't allow anything in your home or church which will entice your children toward darkness. Fill their lives with Jesus, the Word, and Christ, the anointed One, and the Holy Spirit, the anointing.

Children and Revival

God gave the fivefold ministry gifts to heal, grow up, and strengthen the saints (children included) so they (children included) could do the work of the ministry. It is our deepest desire that you will see the importance of children in the Body of Christ and make them welcome, in your home and the church, so they also can be equipped to do the work of the ministry.

Kathy and I believe strongly that children will have an important part in the revival which is upon us. This is the beginning of the final outpouring of the Holy Spirit mentioned in the New Testament and the book of Joel. However, with this belief is an equally strong sense of responsibility to see the next generation saved, filled with the Word of God, and walking in the power of the Holy Spirit.

Whether you are a parent, children's minister, or simply a member of the Body of Christ, this book is not just a "how to" book, but a prophetic call to our generation to reach the next generation.

This upcoming generation has been labeled "Generation X" by the world, but that "X" turned around by Jesus becomes a cross! I believe the children in your home today could be the last generation before Jesus returns. They are marked for God!

> **And they that shall be of thee shall build the old waste places: thou shalt raise up the foundations of many generations; and thou shalt be called, The repairer of the breach, The restorer of paths to dwell in.**
> **Isaiah 58:12**

We can see from God's Word that it is our job to take children into a relationship with the Father, Jesus, and the Holy Spirit. We must make the child feel totally welcome, which makes Jesus welcome, and then God is pleased and the Holy Spirit is free to move powerfully in their midst.

Chapter Three

Standing on the Word and Pouring in the Oil

Genesis 18:19 says Abraham was blessed, not because he was a good businessman, not because he was a good tentmaker, not because he was the best farmer, lawyer, banker, doctor, architect, or salesman, but because he taught his children and his children's children the Word and commanded them to keep it.

Why did Abraham and God put such value on this? Because knowing and keeping God's Word bring divine protection into your life. When I would go hunting for rabbits with my dad, there was one place they could go where we knew we couldn't get them — the thorn bushes. Even if we shot the rabbit, to try to reach through the thorns to get the rabbit out was far too painful and troublesome.

When you teach and command your children in God's Word, you are literally building a divine hedge of protection around them. Like a rabbit who runs into the thorn bushes when the hunters come, your child will run into God's Word and the power of the Holy Spirit at the first sign of temptation, trial, or trouble.

> **Keep thy heart with all diligence; for out of it are the issues of life.**
> **Proverbs 4:23**

> **For as he thinketh in his heart, so is he.**
> **Proverbs 23:7**

Proverbs also tells us that foolishness is bound in the heart of a child (see Proverbs 22:15), and only you, the parent, can protect their heart. In our parenting classes, concerned parents often ask, "To what extent does it become religious or legalistic to monitor television programs and therefore guard the hearts of our children?" The Holy Spirit gave me this picture as an answer to that question.

If you had a rattlesnake loose in your home, would you just go to sleep and do nothing or would you kill it and get rid of it? Spiritually speaking, the TV has the potential to cause much more destruction than a rattlesnake! Selah (Think about that!)!

The Challenge

We challenge you to turn off your TV for one month and have family Bible study and praise, or fun and games. After a month of having the Word pumped into you and getting to know your family better, make a quality decision about what should or should not be allowed into your home.

If you fathers especially want the blessings of Abraham, teach the Word and then guard the Word of God that He deposited in your family's heart as though by a "hedge of thorns."

> **When a strong man armed keepeth his palace, his goods are in peace.**
> **Luke 11:21**

Proverbs 11:16 says that a strong man retains his riches. He guards them. He builds a wall around them like a castle. After all, a man's home is his castle.

There are three typologies of the Body of Christ with Jesus as the head presented in God's Word: Jesus and His bride, the shepherd (pastor) and his sheep (congregation), and the husband and his wife and children. With this in mind, when we observe scriptures that pertain to a pastor, we also can apply the same principles and message to the family.

We can look at 1 Timothy 4 not only as the Holy Spirit's exhortation from Paul to Timothy but also apply it to our families.

> Now the Spirit speaketh expressly, that in the latter times some shall depart from the faith, giving heed to seducing spirits, and doctrines of devils.
>
> 1 Timothy 4:1

This scripture indicates not all, but some will leave the faith. What is **the faith**? **The faith** is all of the Word of God, the whole counsel of God, or sound doctrine. Abraham was blessed because God knew he would teach his children and grandchildren and guard the Word in their hearts.

As the verse continues it says they'll give heed or listen to seducing spirits and doctrines of demons. In verse 6 it says,

> **If thou [men put children in remembrance] put the brethren in remembrance of these things [the Word], thou shalt be a good minister [mighty man, a good father or mother] of Jesus Christ, nourished up in the words of faith and of good doctrine, whereunto thou hast attained. (Brackets mine.)**

The Greek word translated **remembrance** was an architectural term meaning the "jacking up of the foundation and pushing back the foundation that slipped out." Jesus (the Word) is the cornerstone. The cornerstone is the starting place, or foundation, of a building. Jesus is to be the cornerstone, or foundation, of our lives.

Through humanistic teaching, the world has shoved the foundation (the Word) out from under our temples (children). So in 1 Timothy 4:6 the Holy Spirit says, "Jack them back up and shove the foundation, the cornerstone, Jesus, the Word back under them."

The Holy Spirit continues to bless the pastor and/or the parent who obeys and completes this spiritual renovation.

Chop It Up

We've made a big issue of you teaching your children the Word, because it's a big issue to God. But you're probably asking yourself, "How can I do that? I'm not called like Rich and Kathy. And I thought that was the childrens minister's job, anyway." Isaiah 28:9-11 says:

> Whom shall he teach knowledge? and whom shall he make to understand doctrine? them that are weaned from the milk, and drawn from the breasts. For precept must be upon precept, precept upon precept; line upon line, line upon line; here a little, and there a little: For with stammering lips and another tongue will he speak to this people.

These verses tell us first *who* to teach, **them that are weaned from the milk, and drawn from the breasts.** That verse reinforces Matthew 18 and 19, which tell us to teach young children.

Second, we are told *what* to teach. We are to teach them **precept upon precept; line upon line,** which literally means the "deep truths of God." Little children can receive and understand the deep truths of God's Word!

Third, God does not leave us hanging. He goes on to say *how:* **here a little, and there a little.** You teach children like you would lay brick for a home, brick by brick, here a little and there a little. Wherever you are, whatever you are doing, there is no life experience in which the Word cannot apply.

Matthew 18 and 19 and Isaiah 28 say that you need to teach your children God's Word a little bit at a time and apply it to whatever is going on in your lives. But how do you actually tell them? Chop it up!

A baby cannot eat a whole apple, so what do you do? You chop it up until it becomes a consistency the baby can chew and digest. You feed a baby applesauce until he or she gets old enough to eat pieces of an apple, and then the whole apple. A young child can chew and digest a hamburger, but not a steak. Hamburger is ground up, chopped up steak. Same food, but easier to eat.

What to Teach

Teach your children how to use their Bible. Teach them the books of the Bible, the difference between the Old and New Testaments, and how to find specific verses for the situations that concern them.

Most importantly, tell them what God has and is doing for you and in you. Too many parents hide their struggles from their children, giving them the false impression that a good Christian is a perfect Christian who has no temptations or troubles in life. But if you teach them the Word God is teaching you, as well as the Word they need for their daily walk, then your children will grow up to know how to read and search out Scripture themselves, following your example.

As you do this, teach your children who God is: His character, His ability, His faithfulness, His unchangeability. Teach them that God loves them regardless of any mistakes they make. Tell them stories of the saints of old, pointing out how God was faithful, merciful, or just. Tell them about great men of our time like Smith Wigglesworth, Oral Roberts, and others. And most of all, tell them their family members' experiences with God.

Read Psalm 78 to your children, which I call a book of remembrance. The main theme of this psalm is that the people of God sinned when they forgot what God had done for them. Remind your children of all the miracles and blessings God has bestowed on your family as you read about Him doing the same for the Old and New Testament saints.

Stories about real people, both past and present, will reinforce their trust by showing them God really works in people's lives. When you teach your children God's character, they will learn to trust Him and His Word. The Bible says in Psalm 9:10 that those who know Who God is — His character — will put their trust in Him.

When Kathy had to have knee surgery, we asked friends whom we trusted to recommend a doctor. You don't go to a doctor you don't trust. You want to know his qualifications, his reputation — what his name stands for. Similarly, you don't take your car to a mechanic unless you have friends or family who have been treated fairly both mechanically and financially by the recommended mechanic. You want to know they have a "good name."

In the same way, you can't expect kids to trust or live for a God they don't know, not to mention a God they believe does not heal, deliver, guide, or provide. But if you allow God to be your healer, deliverer, guide, and provider, and you encourage and teach them to do the same, they will love Him and trust Him. As they see God show Himself strong for you and for them, God's name — what He stands for — will be a real and vital part of their lives forever.

The Names of God

One of the ways you can teach your children to know God is to teach them His names. Actually, God has many names, and each one reveals an exciting aspect of His character and how He wants to bless us. Following is a fun way of teaching your children twelve of the Hebrew names of God. God's names give us tremendous insight into who He is and what He wants to do for us.

Jehovah Tsidkenu:

He sits in my canoe and makes me look real good.
He is the God of righteousness.
He has made me righteous.

Jehovah Rohi:

He "rows" my boat in the right direction
He's my leader,
He's my shepherd,
He talks to me.

Jehovah Rapha:

He heala my cougha.
He's my healer.

Jehovah Jireh:

He won't make you crya,
He's your provida,
He gives ya everything ya needa.

Jehovah Nissi:

He ain't no sissy,
He always causes me to win,
He's my victorious warrior,
He's my banner.

Jehovah Shalom:

He brings peace to my home,
and wherever I roam,
He's the God of peace.

Jehovah Shammah:

He's better than your momma,
cause he will be with you wherever you go.
He is the Omnipresent,
the guiding and guarding presence of the Lord.

Jehovah Gmolah:

He give ya more mulla,
than the devil stola,
He's the God of repay, otay?

Jehovah Makkeh:

He maka the devil,
shut uppa his moutha,
He's the God that smites my enemy.

Jehovah Hoseknu:

He makes all things brand new,
He's the Lord God Creator.

Jehovah M'Kaddesh:

He pours out His Spirit,
on the old folks,
and on the kiddies,
He's the God that anoints me.

Jehovah Elyon:

You don't have to yell up yonder,
He's here,
But He's also way up yonder,
He's the Most High God.

These names become real to you and your children as you apply them to the various situations you are facing.

What else should you teach them? Teach them the devil would like to use them for a punching bag, and that they need to become like a greased pig. A greased pig? What?! Let me explain.

Greased Pigs

Proverbs 24:16 speaks of how a righteous man can fall seven times and still rise up again. When I studied that, the Lord gave me a picture of Christians being "punching bags" at which Satan throws his blows of sin, poverty, sickness, and defeat. But each time we go down we rise up again. Just as the weight in the bottom of a toy punching bag brings it back up, so the Word in us brings us back up after each blow from the devil.

In the first part of this chapter, we have seen how the Word is our anchor in life, but there is another element we must teach our children and have in our lives to empower us and sustain us. We must not only stand on the Word, we must teach our children how to receive the pouring in of the oil — the mighty power of the Holy Spirit.

One day God gave me the idea of pouring oil, which is a symbol for the power of the Holy Spirit, over a punching bag, then having a child try to hold it down. The oil makes the punching bag slippery and impossible to hold down. Likewise, when we pray in tongues, it's as though the Holy Spirit pours oil all over us, protecting us, so ol' ugly face can't hold us down.

As a young boy on the farm, each year we'd go to our county fair. They would have a "greased pig" contest. A pig would be smeared from one end to the other with lard. Then it was let out into a pen with ten to thirty young farm boys who would try with all their might to catch him. It was hilarious! They'd try and try and try and they would end up with as much grease on them as the pig.

As we pray in tongues, we are like "greased pigs" to the devil. Not only that, but everywhere we go and everything and everyone (sinner or saint) we touch gets the Holy Spirit's oil (anointing) on them.

And just as we laughed at the contestants trying to catch the greased pig at the county fair, I can picture God in heaven and the Hebrews 12:2 **cloud of witnesses** in the grandstand laughing as we grease ourselves by praying in tongues and the devil tries in vain to catch us, failing every time. Psalm 2:4 tells us that God sits and laughs at the devil's attacks.

Standing on the Word and Pouring in the Oil

When we were children's pastors in Tulsa, we had the privilege of getting to know many wonderful families. One of them showed us a powerful example of how to teach your children the power of the Holy Spirit in their lives. Unfortunately, it was at the funeral of the mother.

Her young adult son, Jonathon, requested to do part of the eulogy, which was unusual, but Jon is unusual! First, he said that he never heard his mother say an unkind or negative word, and Kathy and I never did either. But then he told something that caused us all to stop and wonder.

Jonathon said that when his mother went home to be with the Lord, he soon realized that he would have to get an alarm clock. You see, she had awakened him every morning by rubbing his head, shoulders, back, legs, and feet — all the while praying in tongues and praying the Word over him.

Kathy and I looked at each other and smiled. This precious mother had understood the principle of the greased pig! And we had another key to why this young man was so strong in God and so incredibly gifted. To be honest, we know very few young men as outstanding as Jonathon.

Teach your children the Word to give them stability and "grease" them with the Holy Spirit every day before you send them off to school or to play. Teach them to "oil" themselves continually by praying in the Spirit. If you have oil on you and shake hands with someone without oil on them, what happens? They get oil on them as they touch you. Everyone your child sees and touches will sense the presence and the power of the Holy Spirit in their lives!

If you remember Carman's song, "Some-O-Dat," the key phrase is, "I don't know what you got, but I sure want 'Some-O-Dat.'" As your children go to school, and as you go to your workplace, become an oiled punching bag, a greased pig! Everyone will see you slip out of Satan's snares and will say, "I don't know what you got, but I sure want some of that." Micah 7:8 says,

> **Rejoice not against me, O mine enemy: when I fall, I shall arise.**

The Hebrew language draws a picture of how a fishing bobber always pops back up after it's pulled under. There is air in a bobber, which causes it to rise above the water. Water reminds us of where sin belongs. Micah 7:19 says that God throws our sin into the sea of forgetfulness. Therefore, when Satan tries to drown us in our sin (or our problems as a result of sin), as we pray in tongues, the wind of the Holy Spirit raises us up, far above defeat.

Teach your children about the Holy Spirit and make sure they have a proper foundation in the Word of God by chopping it up and feeding it to them one bite at a time. Then, when the world tries to push the foundation out from under them, they will know how to trust God and His Word and tap into the presence and power of the Holy Spirit. They will do great exploits for God!

Chapter 4

No Praisey — Go Crazy

We have only touched on the subject of praise and worship so far, but this is one of the most important aspects of bringing your children into an intimate relationship with the Lord. This is also probably the easiest to teach, because today we are surrounded by music at home, in the car, and everywhere we go.

> **I will bless the Lord at all times: his praise shall continually be in my mouth.**
> **Psalm 34:1**

Not only can you have a time of praise and worship during family devotions, but you can sing praises in the car, play praise music as they play or do homework, and even have bedtime prayer and go to sleep with sweet worship music playing. Your example of singing praises to God and worshipping Him all day long is a powerful example to them, but always invite them to join you and encourage them to experience the presence of the Lord for themselves.

King Nebuchadnezzar

You must also *teach* the power of praise and worship. Simply put, a mouth that is continually singing the praises of God means the heart is filled with thanksgiving. Someone who praises God has a heart of gratitude, and if you have a heart of gratitude, you will always be on solid, safe ground.

> **Finally, my brethren, rejoice in the Lord.
> ...it is a safeguard for you.**
>
> **Philippians 3:1 NASB**

If you read the story of King Nebuchadnezzar in Daniel, chapter 4, you'll find that King Neb (Hartman Translation) went crazy because of pride. He would not praise God for his blessings or even recognize that God had anything to do with his success.

The king declared that he had built Babylon by his power and for his glory. He exalted himself, trusted in himself, and gave no thanks or glory to God. Wrong! Therefore, he was abased to the point of living and looking like a wild animal, eating grass in the forest.

When he came to his senses, he began to praise the Lord. Immediately he was restored to his kingship. (See Daniel 4:34-37). He declared that those who walk in pride, refusing to thank and praise God, will come to ruin.

Praise is simply living a lifestyle of continually acknowledging who God is and that we can't do anything without Him. Praise is thanksgiving and trust.

> **Out of the mouth of babes and sucklings hast thou ordained strength because of thine enemies, that thou mightest still the enemy and the avenger.**
>
> **Psalm 8:2**

Psalm 8:2 is a picture of us trusting God as a baby trusts his parents. This is total dependency. This trust strengthens us and stops the enemy.

Remember Jonah and the whale? When Jonah sinned and disobeyed God's will for his life, he was relying on self and the fruit was disastrous. Jonah finally came to himself, and he was delivered when he began to praise the Lord. (See Jonah 2:7.) Praise is simple baby-like trust, and trust brings deliverance!

Remember the names of God from chapter 3? Proverbs 18:10 says, **The name(s) of the Lord** (His character) **is a strong tower: the righteous runneth into it, and is safe.** The righteous run to, call on, and praise the names of the Lord and are safe. Praise and worship are so easy and exciting when you praise God by all His different names, because each name represents a unique way He blesses you.

Praise Is Learned

The Word of God clearly tells us that praise (trust) brings deliverance and safety. We must teach this to our children repeatedly. Praise is learned! In Psalm 89:15 it says that those who learn to praise God are blessed. Just as a child learns to read, write, and do arithmetic, they must learn to praise God.

Here are some key points to teach children concerning praise:

➤ **Praise stops the enemy.** (Psalm 8:2.)

➤ **Praise is trusting God** like a baby trusts a parent. (Psalm 8:2.)

➤ **Praise is learned,** and the learner is blessed by doing so. (Psalm 89:15.)

➤ **God lives in our praises.** (Psalm 22:3.) God is at home and He can be Himself as we praise Him. Jesus came to give us life and to give it more abundantly (see John 10:10), and He does this as we welcome Him in our temple with praise.

➤ **Shout!** (Joshua 6:5.) To shout means to shout. It means to shout with joy in a warlike manner over a conquered enemy. It means to shout loudly, as to split the ears open with sound — not a wimpy shout. This was done in obedience by faith, not by what was seen in the natural. In Joshua 6:10, when Joshua commanded the people to shout, Jericho's walls fell down. In Sunday school or children's church, have the kids name walls in their lives and then corporately shout them down!

➤ **Corporate praise is led by a leader.** Teach kids to respect and respond to the praise and worship leader. When King Jehoshaphat praised God and led the people in praise, they received a miraculous victory and deliverance. In 2 Chronicles 20:18, he bowed down with his face to the ground and worshipped. This was *qadad,* which means "to bow down or surrender." King Jehoshaphat surrendered to God, and as the leader goes, so go the followers.

➤ **Praise and worship leaders are appointed by God.** In 2 Chronicles 20:21, the king, by the Holy Spirit, appointed the praise and worship team. Praise and worship leaders must meet two qualifications: They must be called by God, and they must be found faithful. (See 1 Corinthians 4:2.)

➤ **God expects praise and worship leaders to study and be prepared.** It is not necessary that they be exceptionally talented. Psalm 33:3 says, **Sing unto him a new song; play skilfully with a loud noise.** To **play skilfully** means "to practice, to make or become well, to sound beautiful." This is reinforced by Psalm 89:15, which tells us we can learn to praise God.

➤ **Praise is a choice.** King David said, **I will bless the Lord** in Psalm 34:1 and Jonah said, **I will sacrifice,** in Jonah 2:9. God won't make us praise Him. In Deuteronomy 30:19, He said "You choose." Paul said in 1 Corinthians 14:15, **I will sing with the spirit,** and I will sing with the understanding also (in English and in tongues).

▶ **Praise purifies our minds.** Proverbs 27:21. It's hard to keep your attention on sin when you are focused on Jesus and praising Him with your whole heart.

▶ **Praise brings deliverance from bondage and blesses others.** In Acts 16, when Paul and Silas praised God, not only were they set free, but others were physically and spiritually freed!

▶ **Corporate praise brings unity and strength.** In Psalm 34:3, it says, **O magnify the Lord with me.** The Hebrew word for **magnify** actually means "a twisted thread." You are like a thread who, by yourself, are weak. But when other single, weak threads come together with you in praise, you are all wrapping yourselves around Jesus, becoming strong in Him.

▶ **Praise dresses you right.** Psalm 33:1 says, **Praise is comely for the upright.** The word **comely** means "suitable, right, or fitting." Picture a person dressed in an extremely small or large coat. They couldn't function properly and would look very strange. An unbeliever would look out of place in a **garment of praise**. But a saint with a "garment of heaviness" on would look out of place. David told Saul, "This armor doesn't fit, and I can't fight in this." (See 1 Samuel 17:39.) The **garment of praise** fits us perfectly and makes us look good in God's eyes.

These are key points from the Word of God that children must be taught over and over. As you teach them to praise and worship God, blessings and security will manifest in their lives.

Also, as you sow seeds (teach) on praise and worship, these seeds will grow and bear tremendous fruit — the fruit of the Spirit and the gifts of the Spirit — because God can be Himself!

Praise Clears the Air

Praise and worship are vital in bringing children into the presence of God. After praise and worship their ears are open to receive the message presented. Praise and worship serve to purify the heart and cleanse the mind so we can clearly see by our spirit and hear the voice of God. Children need this cleansing just as much as adults.

God gave the gospel singer, Carman, a wonderful analogy of this truth in the natural. When we walk into church, it is as though the whole building is filled with smoke and fog. The smoke and fog represent sin and worldliness we may pick up while we are out in the world. Our corporate praise and worship in church or in our home are like many powerful fans that blow the fog and smoke away, bringing fresh air (the Holy Spirit) into the room.

Since **where the Spirit of the Lord is, there is liberty** (2 Corinthians 3:17), it is then that we are able to see and hear unhindered. We are able to receive the Holy Spirit's message to us through our pastor or our family members and receive forgiveness, healing, and strength to go out into the world again.

This is especially true in your home. When your children get into a fight and the home is in chaos, call everyone together and praise God until the atmosphere of chaos turns to an atmosphere of peace. Then you can see and hear; you can deal with the conflict according to the Word and by the leading of the Holy Spirit; and peace and joy are restored.

As an adult, you realize what music has done for you, good or bad. Not only does praise and worship music break down spiritual walls in church, but tunes you love help to get you through the struggles of everyday life. Children are no different. Get them "hooked" on good praise and worship music early. (We suggest recordings by Ken Blount and Joey G., as well as our own, "I'm Free," "P 4:8 Space Cadet," and "Saveda Ma Soul.")

In 1983, Kathy and I were going through some really rough times. There were many times when we'd stand in a circle with our kids and just play whatever song was ministering to us at the time. By the time the song was over, the spiritual oppression would lift. We can achieve the same result with praise and worship in our home, Sunday school, or children's church. Then the Word we teach will be planted deep into the hearts of the children before they go back out into the world.

We mentioned that praise purifies the mind. (See Proverbs 27:21.) A good illustration that parallels that thought can be drawn from the story of the battle between the French and the English, when Napoleon and the Duke of Wellington "duked" it out.

The battle was being fought in France. A coded message was being flashed across the foggy English channel to the nervously waiting English mothers, grandparents, and children. The message was deciphered: "Wellington defeated...Wellington defeated...Wellington defeated." The English families were saddened, but as the sun arose, the fog dissipated, and to the delight of the British people the message was clearly seen: "Wellington defeated Napoleon."

That's what praise does to our foggy minds! It raises the "Son" up higher and higher, allowing us to see the truth, not "Jesus defeated," but, "Jesus defeated the devil!" Praise and worship bring children closer and closer to the Lord, because as they spend time in His presence, they learn who He is and what He wants to do in their lives. Teach them to worship!

Chapter 5

Wisdom

———————————→

Wisdom without the "W" (the Word of God) spells "is-dom"! Without the hearing and the doing of God's Word, which is wisdom, you and your children "is dumb." In other words, it's not just what's taught, but what's caught!

A friend told me about a funny experience she had at her parents' home recently. Her children, two of her sisters, and her parents were discussing a controversial subject at the kitchen table one morning. My friend put her hands behind her head as she thought a moment, and looked over to see her father doing exactly the same thing. She saw for the first time that she had done this all her life and never realized it was something she had always seen her father do — until that moment.

The lesson we learn from this is that children are not going to *listen* to us as much as they are going to *imitate* us. Teaching them the Word will mean nothing to them if they don't *see* us doing the Word. That's being a witness to your children so that they can be a witness to the world. That's wisdom.

First Corinthians 3:16 says, **Know ye not that ye are the temple** (or house) **of God, and that the Spirit of God dwelleth in you?** Proverbs 24:3 says, **Through wisdom is an house builded.** If God tells us we need His wisdom to build our spiritual temples, then we need to know what wisdom is, how to get it, and how to apply it. Take note that the words **wisdom (wise)** and **house** are both found in Proverbs 24:3 and in Matthew 7:24-27. Matthew 7:24-27 defines what wisdom is:

> Therefore whosoever hears these sayings of mine, and doeth them, I will liken him unto a wise man, which built his house upon a rock:
> And the rain descended, and the floods came, and the winds blew, and beat upon that house; and it fell not; for it was founded upon a rock.
> And every one that heareth these sayings of mine, and doeth them not, shall be likened unto a foolish man, which built his house upon the sand:
> And the rain descended, and the floods came, and the winds blew, and beat upon that house; and it fell: and great was the fall of it.

Simply put, a wise man is one who hears and does God's Word, or we could say a wise man is a witness, one who acts like Jesus and does His Word. Wisdom is the ability to hear and apply the Word of God to our lives.

Work, Work, Work

God also points out in Matthew 7:24-27 that being wise is work. In Luke 6:48, part of the same story of Matthew 7:24-27, it says that the wise man **digged deep.** To dig a foundation for a home requires much hard work. It took a lot of effort to build that house on the rock, and it takes just as much effort to study God's Word and then act on it.

The Bible says in Matthew 22:14, **Many are called, but few are chosen** — probably because of the fact that it requires work! In the natural, if you did not work, you would not have a house or an apartment to live in. Spiritually speaking, we are building homes too. Again, Proverbs 24:3 says, **Through wisdom is an house builded.**

If God says we need wisdom and Matthew 7 tells us that wisdom is the ability to do God's Word in every area of our life, then we need to know how to get wisdom. James 1:5 tells us how:

> **If any of you lack wisdom, let him ask of God, that giveth to all men liberally, and upbraideth not; and it shall be given him.**

How simply can that be? If you don't know what to do or how to do it, just ask God.

Don't Be a Moron

In Matthew 7, the Greek word for **fool** is "moros," which is where we get the word "moron." So one who hears the Word of God but does not act on it is a moron. What God is saying in James 1:5 is, "If you've been acting like a moron, ask Me and I will give you wisdom, the ability to hear and do My Word."

He goes on to say that not only will He give you the ability not to be a moron, but He will give it liberally. He will pour it out on you. Next He says, He won't **upbraid** you, rebuke you, or put you down. God is saying, "You feel like a moron, I know, but, I'm not going to condemn you! Just humble yourself and acknowledge Me. Acknowledge that you can't make it on your own, and know that with My help you can! And I will give you the power to be a doer."

This same concept is mentioned in Psalm 127:1.

> **Except the Lord build the house, they labour in vain that build it: except the Lord**

keep the city, the watchman waketh but in vain.

The word **vain** is the Hebrew word *shav,* which is derived from the word *shoah.* It means "to be destroyed or flattened, as by a storm." Consider the devastation of a hurricane. This is the kind of destruction that comes upon us when we labor in vain, or without the fear of the Lord. When I think of *shoah*, I picture God chuckling, "You think you can do it without Me, I'll shoah you!"

Of course, we know from John 10:10 that Satan, not God, is the destroyer. But what God is saying is that through His wisdom, you'll have a good foundation. Then, when Satan brings a storm, you'll not be destroyed. The Bible says that the fear of the the Lord is where wisdom begins.

Winning Their Minds

How does this apply to training children? God said that if we're wise, if we're a witness to our children, then we can win their minds.

> **He who is wise wins souls.**
> **Proverbs 11:30 NASB**

Through His wisdom we will help build the spiritual foundation of our children's lives.

The old adage "monkey see, monkey do" is true. My friend discovered as an adult that she had been doing what she had grown up seeing her father do. Our actions speak louder than our words. What our children see us do (our witness) they will do.

As parents, we need to acknowledge that we can't raise and train children on our own, and that we are totally dependent on the Lord! True wisdom is acknowledging total dependence on the Lord Jesus.

King David understood this concept. In Psalm 30:10, he preceded **praise** by saying, "Lord, be my helper." In other words, "I can't make it on my own, but Lord, You can do anything. The only way I can make it is with Your help." He followed this statement with praise!

God's Grace

In Luke 1:28 the angel told Mary she was highly favored. The Greek wording here means "divine favor for a special vocation." Mary's vocation was rearing Jesus. The Holy Spirit was telling Mary, "I will give you the grace. I will give you everything you need — supernatural favor — to raise this child."

God is no respecter of persons. (See Acts 10:34.) Just as God gave your pastor the grace gift to minister to his congregation and Mary to raise Jesus, He gives each of us grace to minister to our children and those children in our sphere of influence.

We need to walk in the grace that is in Christ Jesus and not rely on self. In Proverbs 18:2, it says,

> **A fool (moron) hath no delight in understanding (God's Word), but that his heart may discover itself.**

This is a key scripture that separates Christianity from every other ideology. Other religions say: "self can do" and "find yourself." God says, "You need My help!"

> Call unto me, and I will answer thee, shew thee great and mighty things, which thou knowest not.
> **Jeremiah 33:3**

What are those "great and mighty things"? Those creative ideas from God you never heard before. A nugget of God's wisdom. A story. A means of breaking down God's Word and feeding it to your children — anything that will win their minds.

God wants us to have His creativity in rearing our children and directing them in His plan for their life. He's saying, "Take it! I want you to have it! It's yours!" Why? Because He loves children and will freely give His wisdom to anyone who seeks it.

God has given each of us the grace to minister to our children. The essence of this key to childrearing is: You can't raise your child, but with God you can. (See Philippians 4:13.)

Grace is not earned or deserved, but it is to be acknowledged and received freely. Wisdom is like the car: it has the ability to go somewhere, or to be used, but it needs fuel. And grace is the fuel that powers the car to run.

God Is a Rewarder

He that cometh to God must believe that he is, and that he is a rewarder of them that diligently seek him.

Hebrews 11:6

The image here is of a hunter seeking after his prey. He doesn't want to come home empty-handed. God is saying that He rewards us. He will give us His wisdom and creative ideas to win the minds of our children.

In Psalm 62:5, King David said, "My expectation is from the Lord." So call on God and expect! Expect to receive wisdom from God, the ability to do

His Word, the ability and grace to win children's minds and thus see their lives transformed.

> Every good and every perfect gift is from above, and cometh down from the Father of lights, with whom is no variableness, neither shadow of turning.
> James 1:17

The phrase, **neither shadow of turning,** is the picture of an eclipse. God is saying there will be no eclipse between you and Him, nothing blocking you from His wisdom or creativity. Just ask and receive it! You can see that when you ask God, He will give you wisdom, or the ability, to win souls. He will tell you how to go about doing His Word.

Jesus is the same yesterday, today, and forever (see Hebrews 13:8). He's no respecter of persons (see Acts 10:34). This means that if He gave King David and King Jehoshaphat wisdom to win battles, He will give you wisdom too! If He gives the mother and father down the block creativity to win children and make them disciples, then He'll do it for you too.

The Power to Defeat the Enemy

Wisdom is one of God's most powerful weapons to aid us and our children in defeating the enemy. I like what Jesus told the disciples in Luke 21:15. He warned them of the persecution ahead and said,

> I will give you a mouth and wisdom, which all your adversaries shall not be able to gainsay nor resist.

The **mouth** is referring to the speaking of the Word. If you are prayed up and studied up, then out of that abundance you will speak. And what you speak, Satan cannot resist. Ecclesiastes 8:4 says,

Where the word of the king is (the Word of Jesus), there is power.

As you speak and do the Word there is a spirit force that Satan cannot deny or resist, somewhat like an invisible force field that you would see protecting a starship in movies like *Star Wars* or *Star Trek*.

God will give you wisdom to minister in word and in deed (doing the Word), and Satan is powerless. It is so important to bury that deep in your heart, especially in rearing children. Your enemy is not your son or daughter. Your enemy is Satan and his imps! Again, God says the devil cannot deny or resist the force of His power when you are speaking and doing His Word.

Remember, **He who is wise** (speaks and does God's Word and will) **wins souls.**

Tell Them Where to Go and How to Get There

I had a boss years ago, before I was saved, who had a sign on his office wall which read: "Tact is the ability to tell a man to go to hell and make him pleased to be on his way." After I got saved, I thought of a better sign:

WISDOM is the ability to tell a man (woman or child) to go to heaven, and make him happy (at peace) to be on his way.

Chapter 6

The Whack

Traditionally, I believe raising children has been called "child rearing" because that's where you apply "the whack" — the rod of correction — on the rear-end! It says in Proverbs 13:24 that if you love your child you will chasten him:

> **He that spareth his rod hateth his son:**
> **but he that loveth him chasteneth him betimes.**

The word **betimes** simply means "to rise up early and be watchful." You are to watch, look, and seek out any rebellion in your child. Then nip it in the bud. The early bird catches the worm of rebellion. And that worm can rot the fruit, your child.

In some circles, the rod of correction is a controversial subject. But you can look until your eyes fall out and we can guarantee you, you will not find any scripture that says it is against God's law to use the rod! If you found it, it would probably be in the "Book of Hesitations!"

Several years ago we were invited to speak at a church where the associate pastor and counseling pastor asked that I not bring up the subject of the rod in my meeting. I then found out that several families were being investigated for child abuse because they spanked their kids. Their children had been interrogated at school and, therefore, abuse was suspected.

That evening as I ministered, a holy boldness came upon me. As I preached, the Lord reminded me of Daniel, chapter 3, where the three little Hebrew boys refused to obey the law of the government because it defied God's law. They were delivered and their enemies were burned up. I was also reminded of Daniel himself, who was told by a government decree not to pray. (See Daniel, chapter 6.) Again, the law defied God's Word and Daniel chose to obey God's Word. He was delivered from the lions, so don't be "lyin" around with worldly people who give their view of the rod!

Don't Be Ignorant

Kathy and I preach long and hard about the correct use of the rod from God's Word. We believe emphatically that if there is abuse, it is because of ignorance of God's instructions on disciplining in love. If you use the rod in anger, it could end up as abuse. And if you abuse your child, we wholeheartedly believe you should be thrown in jail.

We often hear Hosea 4:6 cited, **My people are destroyed for lack of knowledge,** or ignorance, but the verse goes on to say they were also destroyed because of rebellion against the knowledge they had.

In the following pages we will discuss the why's, how's, and even the where's that apply to using the rod of correction. Kathy and I do not want you to miss this powerful truth.

> **Thou shalt also consider in thine heart, that, as a man chasteneth his son, so the Lord thy God chasteneth thee.**
> **Deuteronomy 8:5**
>
> **My son, despise not the chastening of the Lord; neither be weary of his correction: For**

> whom the Lord loveth he correcteth; even as a father the son in whom he delighteth.
>
> Proverbs 3:11,12

> For whom the Lord loveth he chasteneth, and scourgeth every son whom he receiveth. If ye endure chastening, God dealeth with you as with sons; for what son is he whom the father chasteneth not?
>
> Hebrews 12:6,7

Our relationship with our children is a reflection of our relationship with the Father God. That's why it is important to know how God disciplines us and what His Word says about disciplining children.

> Children, obey your parents in the Lord [as His representatives], for this is just and right. Honor (esteem and value as precious) your father and your mother; this is the first commandment with a promise: That all may be well with you and that you may live long on the earth. Fathers, do not irritate and provoke your children to anger—do not exasperate them to resentment—but rear them [tenderly] in the training and discipline and the counsel and admonition of the Lord.
>
> Ephesians 6:1-4 AMP

Children should be trained by taking time to teach them one-on-one with discipline (the rod) and by counsel and admonition (God's words and affection).

The rod represents the painful consequences of rebellion and sin;

God's Word represents the truth that makes you clean, free, and able to resist evil in the future;

And affection is a reminder that God loves you unconditionally.

I think you can see how discipline can be an extremely significant time in a child's — or an adult's — life! When done correctly, the child draws closer to God, closer to the parent or the one administering the discipline, and gains more understanding and wisdom about his or her life.

Here are some other verses which speak of the rod of discipline and the importance of it:

> **In the lips of him that hath understanding wisdom is found: but a rod is for the back of him that is void of understanding.**
>
> **Proverbs 10:13**

> **Foolishness is bound in the heart of a child; but the rod of correction shall drive it far from him.**
>
> **Proverbs 22:15**

> **A whip for the horse, a bridle for the ass, and a rod for the fool's back.**
>
> **Proverbs 26:3**

Note this: *Never, never, never use your hand to discipline children!*

Discipline should only be administered by the rod. Why? Because God's Word names **the rod**, not the hand or the belt, as the instrument of discipline.

God gave man the creativity to invent the belt for one reason, to hold his pants up. If you have used the belt, ask God to forgive you and then ask your child to forgive you.

God designed your hands to give and receive affection; to eat, write, and work; and to be channels for the anointing of the Holy Spirit as you lay hands on the sick and pray for people. If you have used your hands to discipline your child, repent to God and to your child, and commit to both of them that from this time on you will use the rod.

In the Bible a rod can represent judgment, the Word, or divine direction. The children of God are judged, given wisdom, and corrected by Him, not man's opinion of how a child should act. So in a sense, the rod represents correction from the Lord, and He corrects us because He loves us.

Practically speaking, how does this work?

1. Proverbs 10:13 says that the rod is for the **back** of a fool. The word **back** literally means the middle of the backside of the body, or the buttocks. Where do you use the rod? On the buttocks. The interesting thing about this is that a paddle, belt, or hand can bruise, which takes awhile to heal. But the rod, being round, will sting only.

2. Counsel and admonition are directed toward inward attitudes. When a child is disciplined, they should know what they are being disciplined for. Get out the Bible, show them their offense, and discuss it briefly with them.

If a child is only disciplined by the rod, but never counseled about their wrong behavior, they will become bitter, resentful, and rebellious. If a child only receives counsel and admonition, he will not learn self-control. For discipline to work, both discipline and counsel must be administered.

The goal of discipline and counsel is that the child become self-disciplined as they mature. This is a gradual process supervised by the parent, who is led by the Spirit of God in teaching the Word of God.

After discipline with the rod, allow the child to confess his sin and receive God's forgiveness. Pray with them and love on them. This will release them from any condemnation (see 1 John 1:9) and let them know that their sin has been forgiven and forgotten. They are restored and cherished.

When Is Discipline Necessary?

Children need standards. The parents at home or adults in school or church must set them. Parents should discuss with each other the standards to set for their children. Psalm 133:1 says, **Behold, how good and how pleasant it is for brethren to dwell together in unity!**

To have the direction and power of the Holy Spirit, parents must be in agreement when making the rules of their home. It is not wise to disagree in front of the children, but if you do, make certain they see you come to agreement. This teaches them how to deal with conflict.

(If needed, Mom and Dad should go to another room to discuss the problem privately and come into agreement. Remember to make decisions based upon God's Word and the leading of His Spirit. In other words, PRAY TOGETHER!)

Children need boundaries. Make a list of rules for them to live by. The rules should be general and apply to the whole of life. Below are some good rules to start with. You can use these as a guide and add others to fit your children.

1. Always obey all authority. This includes talking back and whining. (3 swats)

2. Respect others and their property. (2 swats)

3. Always tell the truth. (3 swats)

4. Always speak kindly of others. (2 swats)

Note: Two to three swats are normally sufficient. Ask the Holy Spirit for direction and don't start off with too many rules. You don't want to exasperate yourself and your children.

Write it, speak it, and enforce it! Be clear about the specific discipline for breaking specific rules.

Remember the old black and white movies where a king would speak a law, and then tell his scribes, "So let it be spoken, so let it be written, and so let it be done"? In Daniel, chapter 6, Darius was tricked into making a law that would imprison Daniel. King Darius was bound by his own words. Because they were spoken and written, they were required to be enforced.

So it is with God, He "spoke" the world into existence, then He gave his "written" Word, and then He declared:

> **The grass withereth, the flower fadeth:**
> **but the word of our God shall stand for ever.**
> **Isaiah 40:8**

In other words, He spoke it, wrote it, and enforced it. So write (post the rules at their level of sight on the refrigerator), speak (discuss the rules with your children), and then consistently enforce what you have spoken and written, in love!

Discipline your child privately first, so you do not shame or embarrass them. God doesn't make it a policy to publicly humiliate us. And, unfortunately, there are those who will report you for abuse.

Inconsistency in discipline will train your child in a negative way. When he's older he will believe that he may or may not get a traffic ticket for speeding, he may or may not get AIDS from sleeping around, he may or may not get caught robbing the corner drugstore. Basically, inconsistent discipline causes a person to become deceived into thinking there are no consequences for sin.

Lastly, as we mentioned briefly in the beginning of this chapter, never discipline in anger. It should be discipline, not punishment. If you are angry, walk away for a few minutes. Pray and read the Word until you have peace. Then return in a calm state of mind in which to administer discipline.

Are There Alternatives to the Rod?

The popular method the world is using today to discipline children is called a "time out." It is not found in God's Word, but let's examine it.

When you set a child in the corner uncorrected, the seeds of rebellion are not removed, and so therefore the sin is not removed. Proverbs 22:15 says, "The rod will remove it far from him." Seed produces after its own kind, so if rebellion is not removed, it multiples and spreads like crab grass in your spiritual lawn.

A lady once shared with us about a friend who, before "time out" was called time out, was disciplined in that way. As a little girl the sin she committed was not corrected and she was therefore left with the seeds. The lady shared how this little girl would sit in the corner and daydream during her "time outs." Eventually her daydreams became sexual fantasies, which later in her teens became reality — a life of promiscuity. She was reaping the harvest of seed her parents allowed to grow.

Then there is the "chemical imbalance" alternative to discipline. I call Ritalin the fast food drug of discipline. Ritalin is an easy, quick-fix answer to what is usually a discipline or hyperactivity problem — and it is widely used. At one summer church camp where we ministered, Kathy gave an altar call for kids on Ritalin. Fifty-one of the 228 campers came forward.

Thank God many doctors are now saying what Kathy and I have believed for some time, that most children on Ritalin can and should be free of the drug (a form of speed). Our prescription is as follows:

1. Diet: fruit instead of sugar; lots of veggies.

2. Hyperactivity: channel their adrenalin with an exercise program and sports activities.

3. Discipline: be consistent and thorough.

4. Dose of the Ghost: after receiving their prayer language, kids have the power of God to help them control their body and mind.

5. Direct them to their Destiny. (We'll discuss this in detail in Chapter 9.)

A true healing can occur when parents pray and believe God for their child to behave in a godly manner, discipline them scripturally with the rod and godly counsel, and teach them about the power of God's Word and the Holy Spirit to repulse sin and do what's right.

After teaching this in a church recently, an eleven-year-old boy came up to me and confided to me that he was on Ritalin. He said when he didn't take it, he cussed, threw fits, and was totally out of control. I recommended a new doctor to him, Doctor Jesus, Jehovah Rapha, Who would give him a new prescription — a dose of the Ghost. I told him this medicine would give him the power to control his tongue and his body.

Later that week, the young man came to the church camp where we were ministering and he took my advice. He made an appointment with Dr. Rapha and received his prayer language. From that point on he took no medication, and months later his parents reported he was still in complete control of himself. Praise God for Dr. Rapha!

Like an Election

I have set before you life and death, blessing and cursing: therefore choose life, that both thou and thy seed may live.
Deuteronomy 30:19

Unfortunately, kids on Ritalin are viewed as mentally incapable of controlling their behavior, of making the decision to listen, sit still, or obey instructions. It gives a child the false impression that they cannot control themselves. The Bible contradicts this.

One of the most important principles you can teach a child is that their will casts the deciding vote to agree with either their spirit or their flesh. And most of the time, the spirit and the flesh will not agree, so the decision must be made many times each day, every day.

Teach your children that they *are* a spirit. Their spirit is pure and holy and can't sin if they have been born again. Their spirit looks like Jesus and desires only to please God.

However, they live in a body, which Genesis 2:7 says was made from the dust of the ground, and we know from Genesis 3:17 that the earth (ground) is cursed. Romans 7:18 confirms this by saying that there is no good thing in the flesh. So the flesh is like the devil and only desires to please itself and rebel against God.

Romans 12 tells them they have a mind which needs to be renewed, or taught and trained, to agree with their spirit, which is just like God.

> *The **body** doesn't want to praise God, obey Mom and Dad, obey authority, or refuse to cheat on a test at school;*
>
> *the **spirit**, the "real them," is like Jesus and wants to do only what is right;*
>
> *and the **mind** tells the **will** how to vote, depending on whether it has been renewed by worldly thinking and lusts or the Word of God and the leading of the Holy Spirit.*

Like an election, the majority vote wins. If the mind is renewed with the Word of God and you are prayed up in the Holy Ghost, you will agree with your spirit, stay in fellowship with the Father, and do the right thing. But if your mind is thinking worldly thoughts and your heart is set on selfish pleasures, you will do whatever your flesh feels like doing, walk away from the Father, and sin.

Remember, every time you use "the whack," you reinforce the principle that the child is responsible for their life. They will choose to walk in the spirit or the flesh, blessing or cursing.

Encourage Your Children

Children are discouraged by being punished in anger and being punished constantly. Nagging, yelling, and inconsistency in good discipline can be very discouraging to them. Never being praised can cause them to lose heart and become depressed.

Children are encouraged by parents who are tolerant and understanding. (See Proverbs 31:26.) Parents who are good listeners and take time for their children encourage and build them up. (See James 1:19 and Ecclesiastes 3:3.) Children are also encouraged by parents who are interested in what they are interested in. And parents who consistently express love toward their children greatly encourage them.

Set boundaries and post the rules in plain sight

Never spank for an accident

Always spank for rebellion, disobedience, and disrespect to authority

Make sure they understand their sin

Pray with them

Love them

Spend time playing and laughing with them

Listen to them

Encourage them

Why Is the Whack so Important?

Learn from God's Word and from Eli, who knew his sons were sinning and chose not to restrain them. (See 1 Samuel 3:13.) Thirty-four thousand men of Israel were killed in battle because Eli did not restrain his boys. Whether or not you discipline your child could affect the world!

Chapter 7

No Work, No Eat

There are many books already written on the work ethic found in God's Word. Some of the authors of these books have no idea that the wisdom they stumbled upon, the principles which they have identified as causing one to be successful, are from the Bible. Nevertheless, they have come to understand that the financial world works on one main principle:

> For even when we were with you, this we commanded you, that if any would not work, neither should he eat.
> 2 Thessalonians 3:10

Simply put — no work, no eat!

What's amazing to me is that one of America's biggest voids in child rearing is the lack of teaching on the work ethic, and the Church is no exception. Kathy and I have observed many children who don't make their bed, feed the dog, mow the lawn, or help with the dishes. If they do know how to do these things, when their parents ask them to help, they whine, complain, and even argue and throw fits.

As parents, we know how difficult it is to take the time to teach and train a child to do a task, especially when you are in a hurry to get it done! But it is the parents' responsibility to train their children in the two main principles of a successful work ethic:

First, do the job well; and second, do it cheerfully, as unto the Lord.

Setting the Example

I am so grateful for both my father and mother, Jake and Hilda Hartman, who instilled the work ethic in me at a very early age. As a child I witnessed my parents energetically work — and enjoy it. And I saw the financial prosperity that came to them as the fruit of their labor. Their lives have been an illustration of this scripture to me:

> **But thou shalt remember the Lord thy God: for it is he that giveth thee power to get wealth, that he may establish his covenant which he sware unto thy fathers, as it is this day.**
> **Deuteronomy 8:18**

I have great memories of my parents working long, hard hours on our midwest dairy farm. During planting and harvest seasons, they sometimes worked 120 hours in one week. Did my brother and I sit in the house feeling neglected and ignored, watching TV and munching away on junk food? No! We were right out there with them!

The work was hard at times, but we had fun working with our parents, and the rewards — financially and personally — were more than worth it. Because we shared in the work, we shared in the rewards. By the time I graduated from high school, I had $8,000 in savings and a one-year-old car paid for.

One of the most important parts of my testimony is that I always have paid my tithe and have given offerings to the Lord. Why did I do this? Because my parents did, and "monkey see, monkey do"! Not only that, over and over again our family saw how God rebuked the devourer. (See Malachi 3:10,11.) There was one time that stands out more than any other, however.

During the late seventies and through the eighties, the cattle market took a nosedive, and the farmers were hit hard. By the late eighties, my parents were about $2 million in debt. Farmers all around them were losing their farms, but my parents held onto God's promise that He would provide.

They continued to tithe on whatever income they had and to work the farm as diligently as ever. Not only did they keep the farm, but they paid off the $2 million debt and are now making a profit!

The work ethic my father and mother instilled in us gave me the tenacity and perseverence I needed later in life to go to Bible school while working full-time. Their example still encourages me when the demands of ministry become overwhelming. (When this happens, I remind myself that God has promoted me from harvesting beans to harvesting souls!)

Excellence

If you grew up without an example like mine, you are not lost. God Himself set the standard of excellence and introduced the work ethic in Genesis, chapter 1, when He created and then renovated the heavens and the earth. If you will take a moment to read this chapter, you will notice that everything God did was *good*.

This is a great place to take your children to show them that God does things *good*. Then take them to Ephesians 5:1, where it says that we are to imitate God like children imitate their parents. In other words, we are supposed to do things *good*.

Now when Adam and Eve fell, a curse came into the ground and God told Adam that work would be hard because of it.

> And unto Adam he said, Because thou hast hearkened unto the voice of thy wife, and hast eaten of the tree, of which I commanded thee, saying, Thou shalt not eat of it: cursed is the ground for thy sake; in sorrow shalt thou eat of it all the days of thy life;
>
> Thorns also and thistles shall it bring forth to thee; and thou shalt eat the herb of the field;
>
> In the sweat of thy face shalt thou eat bread, till thou return unto the ground; for out of it wast thou taken: for dust thou art, and unto dust shalt thou return.
>
> **Genesis 3:17-19**

I don't recommend reading this to your kids if you don't have time to tell them "the rest of the story," as Paul Harvey would say. God did not leave us in this terrible shape. When Jesus died on the cross, He took *all* the curses!

> Christ hath redeemed us from the curse of the law, being made a curse for us: for it is written, Cursed is every one that hangeth on a tree.
>
> **Galatians 3:13**

But Jesus never told us not to work! He said that His yoke was easy and His burden was light. (See Matthew 11:30.) So there is a yoke and a burden for believers today, but it is *light*. It does not have to be the incredible struggle and horrendous labor it was before the cross.

We know that Jesus understood the work ethic by the age of twelve. When Mary asked Him why He had not followed the family home from Jerusalem, He answered, "Don't you understand that I must be doing my Father's business?" (See Luke 2:49.)

Jesus' entire life on earth was filled with "doing the Father's business." There were times to rest, times to relax, and much time spent in prayer, but His days were filled with work — work He accomplished with excellence.

There were the times when the disciples acted stupid or said something ridiculous, and that seemed to frustrate Him. And there were the times He became angry at the religious Jews for their hypocrisy. But the Word pictures Jesus doing an excellent job of preaching and teaching, healing the sick, casting out demons, not to mention doing miracles like walking on water and feeding thousands of people with two fish and five loaves of bread!

The Servant's Heart

You are probably reading this thinking, "Yeah, but that was Jesus. He had all that power. And He was in the ministry, and the ministry is not boring like the job I've got."

First of all, full-time ministry can seem glamorous, because the people only see you when you're on a platform preaching or teaching — or acting crazy like Kathy and I do sometimes! You don't see us during the other twenty hours of the day when we are unpacking and packing the trailer before and after the meetings, driving eight to twelve hours to the next meeting, spending hours on the telephone booking meetings for months ahead, cleaning our motor home, making sure we have enough tapes, videos, and books for the next meeting, and praying and praying and praying and studying and studying and studying. It's a lot of work — but we love it!

So how do you do your job well and do it cheerfully, especially if it is boring or something you have no desire to be doing?

Well, I know a guy who never did a thing for himself. Everything he did was for his father. And only once did he ask his father if he could do something else — after all, his father wanted him to die for some pretty disgusting people! Even then, when his dad said, "Yeah, that's what I want you to do," he answered, "Okay. We'll do it your way, Dad." How would you like to spend your entire life doing nothing but what your father told you to do?

> But he that is greatest among you shall be your servant.
>
> Matthew 23:11

Of course, the man I'm talking about was Jesus, and these are Jesus' words. He's telling us the secret to a successful life.

Even the dullest job in the world becomes a joy if the worker is doing the job as an act of love.

It takes work to make a happy marriage. It takes work to raise godly children. It takes work to fulfill your calling in God, whether you are in the garage or in the pulpit. But when you love your wife, you love your children, and you love your Father God, then all the struggle melts away.

This is the heart of a servant.

Teach Them to Be Givers

Another thing my father put into me at an early age was that you gave your all regardless of the rewards. Whether you were doing a favor for the widow down the road or getting $15 an hour baling hay, you did your best. When you have the heart of a giver, God will reward you.

And along with that, you paid your tithe and gave offerings (when you could) — in the lean times as well as the prosperous ones. Behind everything was the understanding that God is the One Who gives you power to get wealth, not the government, not your parents and grandparents, not your company, and not your boss.

These are tremendous secrets to success and fulfillment in life. Even as we write this, Kathy and I are conscious that we must teach Destinee to be a servant and a giver, and to do all things excellently, or she will be clueless when she leaves our home to fulfill the destiny God has set for her.

Teach your children to work — and enjoy it! Give them tasks to perform, some with financial reward and some without. They need to understand that when you are part of a family, you do your part, and you do it because you love your family and you love your heavenly Father.

When you develop and teach the work ethic, you are teaching the child that they are a vital part of the Body of Christ and the world at large. *You are showing them that they make a difference.* You are causing them to develop a servant's heart. And you are putting them in a position to tithe and give offerings, to be givers. Then they can experience for themselves that God is their Source for everything.

Chapter 8

Watch the Watch

A watch represents time. How much time do you spend with your children? More important, how much time are others spending with your children? Who, really, is influencing them?

Proverbs 23:7 says that what a man thinks about is what he will become. I've heard it said that the average American TV is on 38 hours a week, so it stands to reason that the time your children sit in front of the TV will affect what they think and therefore what they become. The time they're at school and with friends will also affect them, good or bad.

On the other hand, the time a child spends with a strong committed parent and in church will give him or her something godly to think about.

> **My little children, of whom I travail in birth again until Christ be formed in you,...**
> **Galatians 4:19**

We've all heard it said, "It's not the quantity of time you spend with your children, it is the quality of the time!" No! That statement does not line up with the Word of God, but is just an excuse for putting other things ahead of the family.

In Galatians 4:19, Paul is telling us that in order for Christ to be formed in someone, someone else is going to be doing some travailing, and travailing takes time and effort.

> **Be not deceived; God is not mocked: for whatsoever a man soweth, that shall he also reap.**
>
> **Galatians 6:7**

A man could argue the law of gravity 'til he's blue in the face, then he could also go to the top of a tall building and jump off. All the waaaay down heeeeee could yeeeeeell "gravity doesn't worrrrrk" and splat — he'll find out it works!

The spiritual law of sowing and reaping is just as real as the law of gravity. And the Bible tells us not to be deceived. If you let your children watch trash on television and play with kids who lie and steal, you are going to get a pretty sad harvest. But if you sow time, godly training, and love into your children, you will reap wonderful results.

A few years ago these statistics were given to me by a minister friend. They are probably worse now:

➤ The average public school spends 45 days a year in one-on-one time with a child.

➤ The average Sunday School teacher has 6 1/2 days a year in one-on-one time with a child.

➤ The average parent spends only 2 1/4 days a year in one-on-one time with their children.

So who's spending time with your children?

Friends and family members, music, sports, Nintendo, and TV weren't even listed. But TV alone constitutes 4 to 8 hours daily in most families.

Ask yourself this question, "If the TV doesn't influence people (violence, sex, etc.) as some freedom of speech activists are saying, then why do beer companies spend millions of dollars to do one 30-second commercial during the Super Bowl?" We should be spending millions on Christian advertising: "God is wiser," and "This God's for you!"

By the time a child graduates from high school, he will have seen over 70,000 murders on television. Remember, God says what you think on is what you will become. Watch violence, think on violence — you will become violent.

Statistics on Television Violence

By the age of two or three, most children regularly watch 26-33 hours of TV each week. Who is influencing your children?

➤ 98 percent of all households have at least one TV turned on an average of 6 hours per day. Who is influencing your children?

➤ In an average evening of television viewing, deadly weapons appear about 9 times per hour. Who is influencing your children?

➤ 75 percent of all prime-time network drama contains some act of physical, mental, or verbal violence. Who is influencing your children?

➤ 40 percent of all prime-time TV shows are considered to be very high in violence. Who is influencing your children?

➤ There are actually more violent acts per hour on children's programs than on prime-time television. Who is influencing your children?

➤ The average child has watched the violent destruction of more than 13,000 persons on TV by the time he is fifteen. Who is influencing your children?

► The typical American child sees 75,000 incidents of drinking by the age of 21. Who is influencing your children?

► 78 percent of parents have used the TV as a babysitter at one time or another. Who is influencing your children?

► By the time of high school graduation, most children will have spent 11,000 hours in school, more than 22,000 in front of the TV, and only 3,744 hours in church. That breaks down to this:

School — 11,000 hours, 458 days, or 1 1/4 years.

TV — 22,000 hours, 916 days, or 2 1/2 years.

Church — 3,744 hours, 156 days, or 1/2 year.

Who is influencing your children?

Kathy and I don't need statistics to show us that TV violence affects children. During our travels and the time we have spent as children's pastors we have come to recognize the children who watch violent cartoons and television programming.

What about sex on TV? Only 5 percent of all sexual relationships shown on television is between married, heterosexual couples. The rest is between unmarried people or people of the same sex. Who is influencing your children?

The "Smurfs" cartoon is fairly old; however, on the cartoon networks they're still showing the reruns. So, let's examine it. There's one girl, no mom, no grandma, only a grandpa and all males. Ask yourself — how did they get there? And what is the show promoting?

As I posed these questions at three separate training conferences, three women came to me and said that they saw an episode where a Smurf boy was made into a Smurf girl by a magical potion. So the Smurfette is a transvestite.

Abraham was blessed not only because he taught his children the Word and commandments of the Lord, but he also guarded as by a hedge of thorns the Word he deposited in his children. Who's influencing your children? Watch the watch!

Powerful Influences

According to God's Word, parents are responsible for teaching their children the things of God and the Word. With divorce and the high cost of living, there is a strain on parents, and godly parents are no exception. Between 50 and 60 percent of all children are from divorced homes, and most parents, particularly single parents, cannot afford Christian education. The world's school system, the public school, which has humanistic curriculum, has most children's attention seven times more than the church.

The picture that all the statistics paint is that we are sending kids to the world to be trained in humanism and ungodly thinking. Proverbs 23:7 says that what you think on is what you will become. We must depend upon God's grace and have faith that He will redeem the time. If ever we needed to hear the direction of the Holy Spirit, it is now. We need to watch the watch.

We must remember the awesome responsibility God has entrusted us with: teaching children. We need to do our best in prayer and Bible study, as well as to be consistent and faithful in spending time with them. The local body of believers has six and a half days each year to win a soul, to influence them, to create a desire and hunger for a sold-out relationship with God, and to direct them to their destiny (Psalm 127:4.) As parents, we need to spend more than two and a half days a year with our children! Watch the watch. Watch who is influencing your child.

It is said that on the average two out of three kids on the streets in the United States are unsaved, 40 million children in the United States have never been to church, and approximately 85 percent of all salvations are before age 15. Ten percent of all salvations are between ages 15 and 30, and 5 percent of all salvations are after age 30. Yet in most churches and crusades, only about 10 percent of the budget is directed to minister to children!

Also, as we travel, we observe that only a small percentage (the most I've counted is ten percent) of children's teachers in the local church are male.

Where are all the mighty men?

The harvest is plenty, but the laborers are few. How about you? Kathy and I constantly ask ourselves, "What is important?" We are continuously making sure our priorities are right. We must say no to many things, activities, people, and relationships, and say yes to Jesus, prayer, study, and time with our children. Where are we spending our time? Watch the watch.

In Luke 6:40, the *Phillips Translation* says,

> A disciple is not above his teacher, but when he is fully trained (an action that will have lingering results) he will be like his teacher.

Your children will only be as turned-on to God, as knowledgeable in the Word, or as wise (doers of the Word) as you their parent, or you their teacher. Your time with them is crucial. In Ephesians 5:15-17 Phillips it says,

> Live life, then, with a due sense of responsibility, not as men who do not know the meaning of life but as *those who do*. Make the best use of your time, despite all the evils of these days.

Let's look at some people in God's Word who were good and bad influences on children.

Bad Influences

> He [Ahaziah] also walked in the ways of the house of Ahab: for his mother was his counsellor to do wickedly.
> 2 Chronicles 22:3

> But have walked after the imagination of their own heart [the children of Israel], and after Baalim, which their fathers taught them.
> Jeremiah 9:14

> And she (little brat) being instructed by her mom, said, give me John the Baptist's head!
> Mark 6:25 (Hartman Translation)

Notice that in each case the wickedness in the child was taught or *caught* from the parent. If you are reading this realizing that you have taught ungodly behavior to your children, or maybe you just got saved and your children are older, don't be discouraged or condemned! Simply repent, receive forgiveness, and ask God to show you how to pray and what to do to change their hearts. Kathy and I have been there! And we know that God truly delights in doing the impossible.

Good Influences

> And the Lord was with Jehoshaphat, because he walked in the first ways of his father David, and sought not unto Baalim.
> **2 Chronicles 17:3**

> When I call to remembrance the unfeigned faith that is in thee, which dwelt first in thy grandmother Lois, and thy mother Eunice; and I am persuaded is in thee [Timothy] also.
> **2 Timothy 1:5**

The word **unfeigned** means genuine, the opposite of a hypocritical faith. You see, Timothy did not see a two-faced Christianity from his grandma or mama. What they preached, they lived. Timothy saw the real thing and went and did likewise. Paul could see the results of their godly lifestyle in Timothy.

Parents and teachers, your labor is not in vain!

> **My beloved Brethren, be** (a command of commitment) **steadfast** (not capable of being moved from this position), **immovable, always abounding in the work of the Lord, knowing that your toil is not in vain in the Lord.**
> **1 Corinthians 15:28 NASB**

Good and bad influences can make a difference in a child's life, but I would like to point out through Ezekiel 30:18,19 and Deuteronomy 30:18,19 that everyone is ultimately accountable for their own walk, you for yours and your children for theirs. Your responsibility is to be found faithful, as mentioned in 1 Corinthians 4:2. We have a responsibility to teach them, but in the end it is up to them to choose to do right. The question again is: Who is influencing your child to do right?

Time with Each Child

I want to share some practical things Kathy and I have observed in counseling sessions with parents with respect to spending time with each child when there is more than one in the home.

Family devotion time, whether ten minutes or an hour, should be a priority. Sing one or two praise songs (use a tape if you are not musical) and one or two worship songs. Pray in the Spirit, sing in the understanding and in the Spirit. (See 1 Corinthians 14:15). We suggest that when children can read, they do devotions. Let everyone take turns.

In addition to devotional time, spend time — ten minutes, thirty minutes, or an hour — with each child individually. Do something of interest to *them*. Use this time to compliment, encourage, and build up your child. Ephesians 4:29 says,

> **Let no corrupt communication proceed out of your mouth, but that which is good to the use of edifying, that it may minister grace unto the hearers.**

The word **grace** means "beneficial opportunities that are understood." If you were a businessman, it would be like someone coming up and giving you a million dollars to begin a new business, with no strings attached. You didn't earn it, deserve it, or ask for it. They just gave the money to you and wanted nothing in return.

That's like the grace of Jesus. He died on the cross before you were even born. He didn't ask if you would want Him to; He just did it. He did it whether you would accept Him or not. That's grace!

Spend this individual time exhorting your child in their gifts and callings. Then once a week spend one to four hours per child, dad with daughter, mom with son, dad with son, mom with daughter, on a special outing of their choice: McDonald's, the mall, skating, biking — a date, so to speak.

On those special outings tell your son to open and close mom's doors, and dads do the same for your daughter. In doing so you will be preparing them for their future mate. They will know what is and isn't proper. They will know what is God's best and will accept nothing less.

It is important that your children spend time with you other than being disciplined and corrected. You should spend some time just having fun, enjoying one another, and sharing desires and dreams. Believe me, if you don't, the enemy will make certain someone does!

Be a good influence on your children — and to children around you who don't have godly parents as your children do.

Watch the watch!

Chapter 9

Hitting the Bull's-eye

> Train up a child in the way he should go:
> and when he is old, he will not depart from it.
>
> Proverbs 22:6

My question has always been, "Why do we see kids depart from God's Word when their parents have used the rod, taught them the Word, and seem to have been godly examples?"

We believe God reveals to us through His Word the answer to this perplexing question. The answer lies in the many meanings of the Hebrew word that is translated **train up**.

Chanak

In the Hebrew language, many times there are several meanings to a word in order to bring clarity to the picture the Spirit of the Lord is trying to paint. The phrase **train up** is the Hebrew word *chanak*, and it is only used five times in God's Word. Its flowery meaning paints several pictures to help us understand how God would have us train up our children.

One of the meanings of *chanak* is to throttle, to govern, to restrain, and to narrow the path traveled. Let me give you a personal example of this meaning.

In the summer of 1981 I moved to Oklahoma and landed a job driving an oil tanker. One day as I was following six or seven other trucks to a location, the governor spring on my Mack truck broke. This meant that my throttle was held wide open. My truck was literally a runaway, traveling hills and curves at more than 65 miles per hour with a load weighing in excess of 120,000 pounds. I was out of control! Not only was I in danger, but so was everyone in my path.

In 1 Samuel, chapters 3 and 4, we find the story of Eli and his two sons, Hophni and Phinehas, who were as out of control as my tanker. The Bible says Eli knew his sons were sinning, but he **restrained them not**. Because this man of God did not restrain, or throttle, his sons, 34,000 of Israel's men were killed in battle.

When Eli heard the news of his boys' death, there is no record in Scripture of his response. But when he heard of the loss of the ark, his ministry, and the anointing, he fell over backward, broke his neck, and died.

Here was a father who obviously cared about the ministry, but not his children. Because he did not restrain them, not only did it cause the death of those children, but their sin affected 34,000 other lives and their family members.

Refusing to restrain your children doesn't just affect your home, it affects the world!

Chanak also means to strangle or choke by the hanging of a rope. Now God is not saying to hang your kids, even though there may be days you feel like it! God is painting a picture of controlling their growth, like pulling back on the reins of a horse with a bit in its mouth.

At the mall you see parents with a "mall leash" on their one- to five-year-olds. Now wouldn't it look foolish if you saw a friend and their 16-year-old son or daughter walking down the mall with a mall leash on them? The point I'm trying to make is that there comes a time when the child should graduate to more responsibility.

There comes a day in the mall when the parent may say, "Here's $3.00. Go over to the refreshment area and get us each a pop." As the child carries out the task, the parent watches carefully. But when the child becomes a teenager a parent may say, "Mom and I are going to Dillard's. Meet us back at the main entrance at 4 o'clock."

The message here is that of a gradual release, giving the child more freedom and responsibility as they are ready. When do you take their leash off? When do you let them shop for themselves? I can't answer that, but the Holy Spirit will tell you!

I will instruct thee, and teach thee in the way which thou (and your children) shalt go: I will guide thee with mine eye.
Psalm 32:8

Another meaning of *chanak* is to inaugurate, to induct or install, or set in position for use in a public office or a military office.

You are training and preparing your child for their specific position in the army of God and the Body of Christ. What has God called them to be? Again, the Holy Spirit knows, and He will tell you and your child what that is.

Chanak also means the dedication, grand opening, or ground-breaking ceremony of a new establishment. There is usually a party or celebration. It's new, it's fresh, it's clean, and it has never been inhabited before.

I think it is no coincidence that in Genesis 2:7 God says we are made from the dust of the earth, and the meaning of **train up** indicates a ground-breaking ceremony!

When malls, businesses, or churches have their grand opening, they advertise it, promote it, and make big banners. They are proud of their new building. They invite friends and relatives and the general public. There's excitement in the air. Often there are celebrities attending.

Then they dedicate the new building to the purpose for which it was designed. It's a big deal! They do whatever it takes to get the community there to use the new building.

Kathy and I were honored when we were invited to be a part of the dedication of friends who pastor in Texas. I want to re-emphasize it is an "honor" to be a part of a dedication, not a burden.

When Kathy and I were building a home several years ago, we dedicated it to the Lord. We wanted our home to be used by God as He willed. We made it a public event and had all of our friends stop by and write scriptures on the studs. The awesome part was that several "beer-drinking, hell-raisin'" men on the construction crew were faced with God's Word every day as they worked!

That's how our children are as we dedicate them to God. All the world can see our "open epistles"!

The word *chanak* is used to describe the dedication of the temple in 1 Kings 8:63 and 2 Chronicles 7:5; and is used twice in Deuteronomy 20:5, where it refers to the dedication of a man's home. Are we not the temple of the Holy Spirit? (See 1 Corinthians 3:16.)

On June 17, 1995, Kathy and I flew from Tulsa to Anhui, Mainland China, to pick up our beautiful 10-month-old daughter. When we arrived home July 2, 1995, nearly 100 friends came to celebrate and dedicate our new little temple, Destinee Quila Hartman. What an exciting day! We are, to this day, continuing to celebrate the joy of our little temple. Our focus as parents is on what God made her to be and how we can help bring out her gifts for the world to enjoy.

When you have a ground-breaking ceremony, you're announcing to the world there's a new building going up. And when a couple has a child, they send out birth announcements. They are saying to the world, "Hey, we've broken ground, we're building a new temple. Come and celebrate with us. We want to show off our new building. It is brand new — fresh, clean, never been inhabited or occupied before."

The parent is to see to it that their little temple is filled with God — His Word and His Spirit. And they ask Him, "What is the designated use of this new building You have given us?" Then, as they grow they are continually throwing a party to tell the world!

So to **train up**, *chanak,* means many important things: to restrain, to gradually release into greater freedom and responsibility, to set in position, to dedicate for a specific purpose, and to celebrate. This is a little more than just using the rod every time your child acts in rebellion!

APE's and TP's

Earlier I talked about children leaning toward the *Son* like plants lean toward the *sun*. All children have a built-in desire to seek the Son for warmth and growth. God put in all human beings the desire to seek Him in the supernatural.

All children have a desire to know Jesus, the Way, but they also desire to know their way, what God has planned for them, His way for their life.

Once when we were ministering, the Holy Spirit had me do an altar call for APE's and TP's. You're probably asking, "What are APE's and TP's?"

And he gave some, apostles; and some, prophets; and some, evangelists; and some, pastors and teachers.

Ephesians 4:11

God has given Apostles, Prophets, Evangelists (APE's) and Teachers and Pastors (TP's) **for the perfecting of the saints, for the work of the ministry, for the edifying of the body of Christ** (v. 12). After I've taught the children about Ephesians 4:11 and God's call on their lives, Kathy comes out with a monkey mask on and a roll of toilet paper in her hand. The kids double over laughing, but they will never forget APE's and TP's (nor will you!).

Once when I asked for those who knew they were called to be APE's or TP's to come down to the altar, 25-30 children (5-12 year olds) came. I prayed for each one, and when I got to the third little girl in line, the Lord said to me, "She's an evangelist." I asked her what God had told her she was. She said, "I'm a missionary and a singer and my mommy and I are going to sing at such and such church next week."

I said, "That's right, God has called you to the mission field." God had sent Kathy and me to confirm the call on her life.

The last two children in line were boys. When I approached them, it was as though God had written "pastor" on their forehead. So I asked each of them,

"What are you called to do?" They both responded immediately, "Pastor."

I looked at them both and said, "That's right, boys, God has called you to be pastors," and we prayed accordingly. The point is that God used us, traveling ministers, to confirm their natural bent, their position in the army of God, their designated use as spiritual temples.

If God would entrust to me a word to confirm their calling, how much more would He use you, the parent, and your ministers, members of your congregation, relatives, and friends? Local people not only can confirm, but over the years can help develop and nurture the gifts and callings in children.

ETC

ETC is an Extremely Trained and Talented Christian. What is an ETC? Those men and women of God who are ushers, greeters, secretaries, Sunday school teachers, nursery workers, praise and worship leaders. They are on the assembly lines and in the executive board rooms, in athletics and the fine arts. They are witnesses for Jesus at work, at play, and to those the pastor and evangelist could never reach.

ETC's also finance the gospel. They finance the APE's and TP's and have an equal share in their rewards for all those who are saved. In our short time as ministers, we've seen thousands of children saved and filled with the Holy Spirit. We have a dentist friend who does our dental work as an offering to our ministry. That man and his family have an equal part in those salvations. We have a CPA who charges us minimal fees to help our ministry. He too has an equal reward in the thousands of lives touched.

In Deuteronomy 8:18, God rebukes the people for being prideful concerning financial blessings:

> But thou shalt remember the Lord thy God: for it is he that giveth thee power to get wealth, that he may establish his covenant which he sware unto thy fathers, as it is this day.

You see, the APE's and TP's need the ETC, and the ETC needs the APE's and TP's.

> And the eye cannot say unto the hand, I have no need of thee: nor again the head to the feet, I have no need of you.
> 1 Corinthians 12:21

Just like all our body parts are necessary for us to function to full capacity, every part of the Body of Christ is important. Kathy and I know a man in the midwest who is an ETC. This man is a CPA and a real estate investor. One time this man (we'll call him Joe) was headed with his partner to buy a business. On the way, the Holy Spirit spoke to him and said, "It's yours, but not now."

Joe told his partner what God had said, and his partner got mad and dissolved the partnership. He convinced some other investors to purchase the business with him. Within a short time that business burned to the ground and Joe went in and purchased the parcel of land for about a dime on the dollar. One year later he turned around and sold the renovated business and profited $1.3 million.

Joe has an anointing to make money. This is his calling. Just as a fivefold minister is sensitive to the voice of the Holy Spirit while teaching and ministers words of knowledge or wisdom, Joe is sensitive to the Holy Spirit's voice concerning buying and selling, organizing, creating, and so forth. Joe knows that his anointing to make money is to finance the Gospel. He can have nice things, but his primary purpose on planet earth is to finance APE's and TP's.

When Timothy's church was facing persecution and having to deal with false doctrines, Paul told him in 2 Timothy 2:1 to **be strong in the grace that is in Christ Jesus.** Grace is unearned or undeserved. God gives me the grace to teach families the Word so they can be healed and be delivered. Joe's grace gift is to make money to finance our ministry and others.

When you know your gifts and callings, you have no need to be jealous of others. You can be excited and love what God has done in you, and you are excited when you see others excelling in their gifts and callings.

Hope

Why is this so important, and how does it shed light on why many children depart from God? The Bible says in Proverbs 13:12, **Hope deferred maketh the heart sick.** The word **deferred** means, "to set aside."

God does not want you to set aside your child's calling.

If they have a desire to make money, be all the more diligent to teach them stewardship, tithing, giving of offerings, and most important, giving glory to God.

A child is no different from an adult. When they lose sight of the vision and desires God placed in them, they become lethargic, depressed, directionless, and an open door for evil devices and deception. I always say that a child without hope turns to dope —

or other things. They need to know their gifts and calling and then strive to attain them. If they don't, they'll become discouraged and give up.

> The steps of a good man are ordered by the Lord: and he delighteth in his way.
> Psalm 37:23

Obviously, if you yourself have no idea what God is calling you to be and do, Kathy and I want to encourage you: You and your children can learn together!

Kathy and I were not saved until we were adults, and we already had children. It took us some time to figure it out ourselves, and as we heard from God about our lives, we began to challenge our children to seek God about theirs. Then we began to see things in our children to confirm what they were seeing and hearing from God. Destinee is still very young, but every day we are seeing her gifts and callings emerge more and more clearly.

> As arrows are in the hand of a mighty man; so are children of the youth.
> Psalm 127:4

Every arrow has a bull's-eye, a target, a destiny, a purpose, a direction to be headed towards. And the Bible says that an arrow is shot from the hand of a mighty man. That mighty man is YOU: the parent, the teacher, the children's church worker, the neighbor. You are the one God has chosen to bring hope to children!

I would like to encourage you, as a member of the Body of Christ, to look at your sphere of influence and ask God to show you arrows who do not have a mighty man or woman to aim them at their bull's-eye.

What is the bull's-eye? Jesus. He is the way, and no man comes to the Father but by Him.

What's the bull's-eye? A child's natural bent or inclination.

What's the bull's-eye? A child's position as a soldier who brings others to Christ.

What's the bull's-eye? A child's designated use as a temple of the Holy Spirit.

Teach them the Word and be a godly example, but equally important, pull their gifts and callings out of them! Give them hope!

How to Take Aim

How do you aim children as arrows to their given gifts, calling, and destiny — their bull's-eye?

The wealthy industrialist Andrew Carnegie was once asked how over the course of his lifetime he had had 37 men to whom he paid over a million dollars a year in salary. He said he "mined men like men mine mountains for gold."

Your child is like a mountain where tons of earth surround the valuable treasures God has hidden in them. I picture the Word as a pick and shovel which digs into the mountain to remove all the hindrances and finds the gold.

Then, to help things along, God gives the Holy Spirit. In the old movies you'd see the miners bore a hole in the side of a mountain, stick some dynamite in, go a safe distance away, and blow out a chunk of the mountainside, making it easier to get to the gold.

> **He that speaketh in an unknown tongue edifieth himself.**
>
> **1 Corinthians 14:4**

The Greek word for **edifieth** is *dunamis,* which is where we get the word dynamite! Your child is like a mountain of foolishness (dirt) and when you pray in tongues, *dunamis,* or explosive power, makes the mining operation a whole lot easier. It blows away the dirt and makes it easier to get to the gold. It makes it easier for you to *see* the treasure.

When Kathy and I first started as children's teachers, we had a precious young boy named Josh, who was one of those active, hyper, restless types. We weren't quite sure what to do with him, so we began praying in the Spirit, asking God for understanding and wisdom. The Lord revealed to us that Josh was just like his father, who was the church administrator. Josh had an administrative gift inside him!

As the Lord directed, we began to plug Josh into administrative positions in our five-year-old class. We began to draw out the gifts in him, using him as an usher, a greeter, an offering collector, etc.

Later, his mom told us what a difference this class made in Josh's life. At this writing, he is working with Campus Life Ministries and was their youngest employee when he began at age fourteen.

When Kathy and I were teaching that five-year-old class, we were totally ignorant that children had gifts and callings, but through Josh the Holy Spirit began opening our eyes.

The first key to aiming a child toward their gifts and callings is to ask the Holy Spirit, the Coach, for understanding and wisdom.

Then Josh had a brother named Jared, who began to develop an interest in farming. He would go to the edge of a field and stand and watch while their neighbor plowed, planted, or harvested. When his parents observed this fascination with farming, they began to purchase tractor, combine, and planter operation manuals.

Jared devoured those manuals and probably knows as much about the tractors he watches as the farmer who operates them. This doesn't necessarily mean that he will be a farmer or a machanic, but it shows he has a natural bent towards farming and mechanical things.

God can and probably will use this interest later in Jared's life, because his parents have encouraged him. In the meantime, God may be using this interest to teach him personal things or simply to keep his mind occupied with godly pursuits.

The second key to aiming a child toward the bull's-eye is to develop their natural interests and gifts.

On the farm as a young boy, my dad had me drive his 21-foot straight trucks beside him when he was operating the combine during harvest. This helped him save a lot of time because he could unload the grain onto the truck while continuing to harvest the crop. If I drove too fast, the grain would spill on the ground behind the truck. If I drove too slow, the grain would unload on the cab of the truck. Either way I'd waste grain.

Dad saw my liking for driving and encouraged me in it. He showed such confidence in me that I became exceptionally good and excelled in truck driving. Years later, I got a part-time job driving for a nationwide moving company. And all of these experiences led to my driving for Carman Ministries in 1988. I started driving his semi-truck, then later drove his bus, and Kathy began driving one of his trucks (she was a truck driver when we met!).

Kathy and I spent over two years with Carman's ministry, which not only gave us a wealth of knowledge about ministry, but opened doors of ministry to children, teachers, and parents for us across the nation and around the world.

In 1990 Kathy began painting clothes for fun. I said she was making "women's tents," like the apostle Paul, but it was an untapped gift we didn't know was in her. She was so good at it, women would come up and literally buy them off her back, so she'd have to make herself another outfit.

After a year she began to do craft shows and the state fair. Then finally she started her own clothing business. God used this blessing to sustain us and bless us — and many others. Through this business we paid the down payment on our new home, one-third the cost of Destinee's adoption, and were able to purchase our motor home, which is now our home on the road. God used that creative gift in her to help bring us to the place of ministry we are in today.

Were Rich and Kathy Hartman called to be truck drivers or clothing designers? No! But God used those gifts and our pleasure in doing them to direct us to our calling.

> **A man's gift maketh room for him, and bringeth him before great men.**
> **Proverbs 18:16**

Look at your own life and your children's lives. Your gifts are not necessarily your calling, but God will use those talents and abilities and interests to get you where He wants you to go.

When God calls us, He gives us the means, strength, power, gifts, grace, and ability to accomplish that calling. You have probably heard, "Where God guides, He provides." It's true!

Avoid Rotten Fruit

> Train up a child in the way he should go: and when he is old he will not depart from it.
> **Proverbs 22:6**

The word **depart** is the Hebrew word *suwr*, which, just like it sounds, means sour, rotten, decayed, rebellious, worthless, unused fruit.

The best way I could describe *suwr* is through something that happened when we were traveling with Carman. We had been on tour for several months and came home to a refrigerator filled with fruit we had forgotten to dispose of before leaving. OOOH!!! Nothing can describe how terrible and disgusting that sight and smell was when we opened the refrigerator door!

You do not want your children, the children in your church, the children in your school, or the children in your neighborhood to depart, to *suwr*! You do not want them to be a stench and a rotten sight to the world. You want them to be a sweet-smelling reminder of the love Jesus.

> For we are unto God a sweet savour of Christ, in them that are saved, and in them that perish.
> **2 Corinthians 2:15**

God commands the Church to train up our children in the way they should go because it is pleasing to Him and because children are His hope to reach the generations to come.

Training up our children is a community event. We are to direct any arrow in our sphere of influence first to Jesus, The Way, and secondly to their way —

their destiny, purpose, and calling. This is hitting the bull's-eye.

We are to bring hope to our children. And then when they are old they will not leave the things of God and be rotten fruit. But they will have such a wonderful smell and look so good, everyone they come in contact with will want to know the One Who made them that way!

Chapter 10

Willingness

Children are like arrows in the hands of mighty men and women. Our hands. They need to be directed to the bull's-eye, their God-given destiny in Christ Jesus. But are you willing to pay the price?

> **A good man leaveth an inheritance to his children's children.**
> **Proverbs 13:22**

> **But if any provide not for his own, and specially for those of his own house, he hath denied the faith, and is worse than an infidel.**
> **1 Timothy 5:8**

If you died tomorrow, what would your children inherit? Money?

If you left your children a $10 million estate, they could spend wisely, squander, or lose it in a year, five years, or ten years, and what would they have to show for it?

Money doesn't buy love, peace, health, or contentment. But if you have taught your children the Word of God and how to hear and obey the voice of the Holy Spirit, they would be able to succeed through bad times or good times, recession, war, depression, epidemic, flood, earthquake, death, and anything else the world could dish out.

Isaiah 26:3 says those who keep their minds stayed, fixed, or glued to God's Word will have perfect peace. Peace includes prosperity, health — everything needed for their spirit, soul, and body. In other words, stability.

> And wisdom and knowledge shall be the stability of thy times, and strength of salvation: the fear of the Lord is his treasure.
> Isaiah 33:6

Ask yourself:

Am I WILLING to do what God has revealed to me?

Am I willing to take time to teach children the WORD, both in my home and at church?

Am I willing to lead my children into WORSHIP?

Am I willing to be a WITNESS to my children?

Am I willing to teach my children the WORK ethic?

Am I willing to use the "WHACK"?

Am I willing to WATCH who's influencing my children?

Am I willing to direct children as arrows to the WAY they should go?

> I call heaven and earth to record this day against you, that I have set before you life and death, blessing and cursing: therefore choose life, that both thou and thy seed may live.
> Deuteronomy 30:19

Willingness

YES! I, _____, am Willing! I choose to be aware every day of those children in my influence, to teach them the Word, lead them into Worship, be a Witness, teach them the Work ethic, use the Whack (only on my own), Watch who's having an influence on them, and direct them in the Way toward their gifts and callings.

If you just made a solemn covenant with God to do this, then you are a MIGHTY MAN WHO HAS AWAKENED!

We pray and believe God that you will succeed in aiming and shooting many arrows to achieve their full potential as children of God. Hallelujah!

References

Hebrew Honey, by Al Novak (Houston, Texas: J. Countryman Publishers, 1987).

All the Divine Names of God, by Herbert Lockyer (Grand Rapids, Michigan: Zondervan Publishing House, 1975).

A Linguistic Key to the Greek New Testament, by Fritz Rienecker (Grand Rapids, Michigan: The Zondervan Corporation, 1980).

Exhaustive Concordance of the Bible, by James Strong (Grand Rapids, Michigan: Baker Book House, 1992).

About the Authors

Kathy lived in California and Rich in Oklahoma when they met at the national headquarters of the van line company for whom they were both driving. During the eight hours they were waiting for their next assignment, they began to talk. They were both Christians, they had both been married before and had children, and God had given them the same verses of Scripture to stand on for their calling into full-time ministry.

Twenty-four hours later, Rich proposed, and they were married within a year. They lived in Tulsa, where they raised five of their nine children, went to Bible school, and Rich worked a full-time job as well. It was during this time of great challenge that they received their call to minister to children and train parents and children's workers.

After their children had all grown, first Rich and then Kathy began to work for Carman Ministries, driving the bus and one of the semi-trucks. They also began ministering to children in churches when they were not on the road with Carman.

In 1989, they formed Kids Around the World (R&K Ministries, Inc.) and went on the road full time in 1990. From 1992 to 1995 they were the children's pastors at Grace Fellowship in Tulsa, Oklahoma. And now they are travelling full time again.

The desire of Rich and Kathy's hearts is to first awaken adults in the Body of Christ to the importance of children according to Jesus' words in Matthew 18 and 19. Second, to teach them how to minister to children in the home, in the church, and in the neighborhood. They believe God's mandate to them is to *Wake up the Mighty Men*, those who have any influence on any child — to direct children to Jesus, their divine destiny, and their role in the Great Commission.

At this writing they have ten children and ten grandchildren.

If you would like to contact Rich and Kathy, please write:

Rich and Kathy Hartman

Kids Around the World Ministries, Inc.

8177 S. Harvard, Suite 727

Tulsa, Oklahoma 74137

or call:

1-800-940-9024

or e-mail:

katwkathy@aol.com